SHIPS OF THE REDWOOD COAST

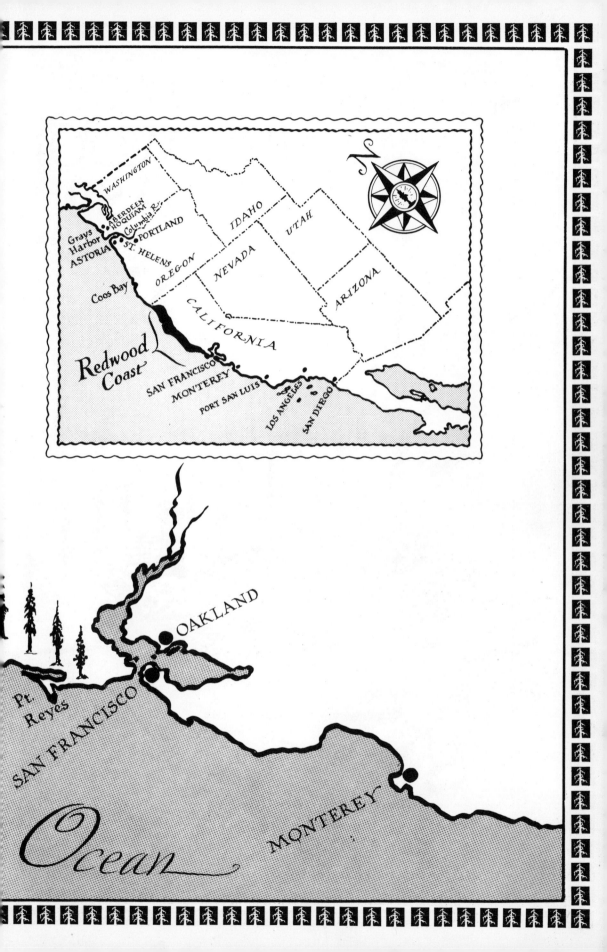

"Standing down the redwood coast"

SHIPS OF THE REDWOOD COAST

By

JACK MCNAIRN

AND JERRY MACMULLEN

Stanford University Press

Stanford, California

STANFORD UNIVERSITY PRESS, STANFORD, CALIFORNIA

Published in Great Britain, India, and Pakistan by Geoffrey Cumberlege,
Oxford University Press, London, Bombay, and Karachi

The Baker and Taylor Company, Hillside, New Jersey
Henry M. Snyder & Company, Inc., 440 Fourth Avenue, New York 16
W. S. Hall & Company, 457 Madison Avenue, New York 22

First printing, October 1945
Second printing, December 1945
Third printing, October 1946
Fourth printing, October 1954

Library of Congress Catalog Card Number: A45-5289

PREFACE

THE idea for this book probably had its beginning years ago, when the little *Svea,* a wooden steam schooner, cut across our bow as we stood into San Francisco. Those of us aboard a big freighter marveled at the *Svea's* huge deck load of lumber, seemingly twice the amount she should carry in safety. Where had she come from? Where did she operate?

Serious thought for such a book began to develop some time later as we steamed up Oakland Estuary toward drydock and spotted the *Svea* laid up in the mudflats. But nothing was done about it until several years later, when a tour of duty in San Francisco presented opportunities to venture over to Oakland and visit the *Svea* and her master, Captain Karl Rohberg. It was undoubtedly the yarns passed along by this venerable old skipper that cinched the idea for a book.

There was little printed information on the old lumber ships, and it was necessary to check over yellowed pages of San Francisco's newspapers of the past. Our heartfelt thanks are extended to the *San Francisco Examiner* and *San Francisco Chronicle* and to the editors of their shipping pages, for it was through this medium that we were able to confirm the identity of many of the vessels, as well as the incidents concerning them.

Grateful acknowledgment is made to Charles R. McCormick, Fred Linderman, Whitney Olson, and Otis Johnson, old-time steam-schooner operators, for their delving into records for factual information. Thanks also are extended such redwood lumber operators as John Ross of the old Mendocino Lumber Company, Clarence Broback of the Union Lumber Company, and Selwyn J. Sharp of the California Redwood Association. Among the others who aided materially were Joseph Moore of the Moore Drydock

Company, K. C. Ingram of the Southern Pacific Company, Professor Emanuel Fritz of the University of California, Judge William D. Vaughn of Mendocino City, Ole Hervilla of Little River, Carl Christensen of Eureka, and E. O. Sawyer, Jr. Acknowledgment also is made to the masters of the redwood ships, notably Captain G. "Midnight" Olsen, Captain Karl Rohberg, and to Captain C. Reiner, Chief Engineer Fred J. Hill, and Axel Reff.

All possible effort has been exercised to prevent mistakes; but, in any word-of-mouth compilation such as this, mistakes may occur. The main purpose in presenting *Ships of the Redwood Coast* is to preserve the story and the history-making events as passed along by the old-time ship operators and masters, who, like their ships, are rapidly becoming a part of the past.

J. McN.

San Francisco, California
  July 1, 1945

CONTENTS

LIST OF ILLUSTRATIONS

The Frontispiece
and the drawings for the chapter heads by
JERRY MacMULLEN

1

PAUL BUNYAN'S COUNTRY

THERE is nothing small about the coast of northern California. It is a region of big trees, heavy breakers, strong winds, and fogs second only to the famous—or notorious—tule fogs of San Francisco Bay and its tributaries.

And yet there was one thing able to exist in this robust area purely because it was small. That one thing was a type of ocean-going vessel which became a dominant factor in the development of the rich timberlands and which played a vital part in the growth of the state. It was small because it had to be; you just don't go puttering around through breakers and into wind-swept dog-holes on the Mendocino shore in a liner or a 10,000-ton freighter —for much the same reason that you avoid driving an automobile through the revolving front door of the Palace Hotel. Along all that imposing stretch of coast, with the exceptions of Humboldt Bay and Crescent City, loading of cargoes is a matter to be attended to within a biscuit-toss of white water boiling over reefs and ledges and with never more than a slightly protruding headland or clump of rocks to give you a bit of shelter. It is dog-hole work, a dog-hole, in case you do not know, being an indentation in a rocky coastline, of course really bigger than an opening into which a dog might crawl, squirm around, and crawl out again, but not much.

The little ship which was born to take on the job of getting millions of board feet of California redwood to the markets of the world was the steam schooner[1]—a thing as uniquely Californian as the Golden Gate, Olvera Street, or the redwoods themselves.

Along that wild coastline thousands of acres of giant California redwoods (*Sequoia sempervirens,* if you want to be that way about it) tower skyward amidst tall ferns, rhododendrons, Indian paint-brush, lupine, queen's lace, and wild iris. It is Paul Bunyan country, and the steam schooner was a maritime version of Paul's faithful blue-eyed ox.

To learn the history of the steam schooner we must turn back the pages of California's history seventy-five years or more, back to the era of the two-masted sailing schooner and the period when San Francisco was undergoing a metamorphosis from an embryonic frontier settlement to an industrial center. Miners coming back to San Francisco from The Diggin's brought stories of redwood forests so dense that sun and rain could scarcely penetrate to the earth; tales of the colossal California forests were carried East by skippers of early-day sailing craft, out of Boston and other Atlantic ports, who had caught glimpses of the towering stands of timber on the cliffs above murky fog banks. Today there are towns and industrial areas scattered through the redwoods, and it is difficult to realize that less than a century ago, roving bands of Puttawott, Weott, Sotoyome, and Wintoon Indians lived there, supporting a lazy existence from the abundant wild life of the forests and the fish of the clear mountain streams.

Russians, part of a group of colonists who had pioneered the Siberian territory, migrated south along the Pacific Coast in search

---

[1] Purists may raise their eyebrows over the term "steam schooner," but they'll never uproot it from the language of the West Coast. And it has a logical foundation, as will presently be revealed.

of sea otters and in 1811 established a trading post at what is known as Fort Ross, some seventy miles north of San Francisco.[2] From trapping they expanded their enterprises to take in general merchandise, and they traded with the Californians, buying grain, hides, and tallow for export to the Russian settlements. They are credited with building the first sawmill in the redwood forests; lumber produced by this water-powered mill was used for building the fort, the cabins, and the church at Fort Ross, parts of which are still standing.

Captain Stephen Smith, master of the bark *George Henry,* visited the Pacific Coast in 1840 and marveled at the vast stands of timber. He also marveled at the lack of imagination which led the local settlers to import their lumber from the Sandwich Islands when there was an unlimited supply virtually in San Francisco's own front yard. Being a practical soul, he shopped around a bit on his next trip home and in 1843 he was back in California with sawmill machinery which he had rounded up in Baltimore. Having located some lumber at Monterey Bay, with the aid of a dozen white settlers from San Francisco he built a sawmill in the redwoods east of Bodega, on Salmon Creek.

A frontier tycoon still earlier was William A. Richardson, an Englishman, who appeared upon the scene as mate of the British whaler *Orion* and settled down at San Francisco—it was Yerba Buena in those days—in 1822. He operated sailing craft along the coast and on San Francisco Bay and became Port Captain, although just what San Francisco needed of a Port Captain in those pastoral days is not entirely clear. Captain Richardson married into a prominent California family, his bride being the daughter of Commandante Martinez.

Eventually Richardson became a man of comparative wealth, his holdings including some 20,000 acres of land, thousands of head of cattle, and several hundred horses. In 1853 he built a sawmill on a river within his land grant on the northern coast, and named the river Albion after his native country; the town of

---

[2] The Russians' fur-trading outposts at one time extended as far south as Guadalupe Island off the Mexican coast, some two hundred miles below San Diego.

Albion, some one hundred seventeen sea miles north of San Francisco, thus became one of the important mill towns of the coast.

A group of Easterners working their gold claim at Rich Bar, now Crescent City, found the going a bit rugged because of the lack of a transportation route to the south which would make the replenishment of provisions possible. And so, in 1848, eight of the miners worked their way toward San Francisco Bay, attempting to find a practical overland route. During their trek, one of the group, David Buck of New York, discovered a large body of water which he named Trinity Bay, afterward renamed Humboldt Bay by a later group of "discoverers," in honor of the early naturalist Baron von Humboldt. Word spread quickly about the rich timber and farming lands bordering this northern bay, and soon families moved into the area which now includes Del Norte and Humboldt counties. Miners who had been professional men found that it was more profitable to cater to the needs of miners than it was to seek gold themselves, and consequently the settlements on Humboldt Bay took on the airs of civilization, with sundry business establishments opening up for serving the inhabitants of the surrounding forests and farm country. These settlements included Union, as the town of Arcata was then known, also Eureka on Humboldt Bay.

It didn't take the frontier settlers long to learn of the values of redwood. Its resistance to fire made it popular for homes and business establishments, and its resistance to decay made it useful for railroad ties, much needed in the early days of railway expansion. An almost inexhaustible supply of redwood at its doorstep, together with the ever increasing demand for lumber, skyrocketed Humboldt Bay to a place of prominence on the Pacific Coast. Lumber soon was being shipped in large quantities to domestic and foreign markets. In 1852, Harry Meiggs, a San Francisco engineer and promoter, loaded a complete sawmill aboard the schooner *Ontario* and shipped it to Big River, the name by which Mendocino City went in those days. At about the same time the R. W. Knox Company of San Francisco shipped another complete sawmill to the north, this one to Crescent City.

Eternal beauty and flitting sunlight in the redwood forests of the Redwood Empire,
California. These great trees, thousands of years old and rising to maximum
height of 364 feet, are the unique inhabitants of a relatively small
section of the earth's surface. Ninety-seven per cent of all
specimens of the *Sequoia sempervirens* live here.

Ox team hauling logs from "skid road" to ship landing.

Two brothers, George and John Cooper, founded a combination flour and sawmill south of Eureka in 1854, the mill operating with some success until 1861, when raiding Indians killed George and set fire to the mill.

Steam-driven mills followed the water-powered ones, and production stepped up considerably. In 1860 California had some three hundred small sawmills operating among the redwoods; by 1885 there were around four hundred of them in the Humboldt forest region, with such mills as the Hume, on Smith River, and Robart's, on the Eel River, turning out better than 30,000 board feet a day.[3]

Railroads, forging steadily ahead into the West, called for vast quantities of redwood ties; the gold rush to Alaska in 1898 and the disastrous fire following the San Francisco earthquake of 1906 further encouraged the establishment of mills.

Redwood, because of its lack of pitch, is a slow-burning wood, and a survey by redwood authorities after the 1906 holocaust at San Francisco brought out the fact that in many instances the redwood siding on San Francisco homes had saved them from destruction by fire. This brought such demands for redwood that the mills were taxed to capacity, and in 1906 an all-time record was set—the redwood mills cut and milled no less than six hundred million board feet of the lumber. Redwood's resistance to fire and decay have been noted; it is also shunned by insects, which makes it further desirable.

The coastal redwoods cover an area some four hundred miles long and roughly thirty miles back from the sea; the redwood tree averages three hundred feet in height and twenty feet in diameter, and attains an age of a thousand years. One may appreciate its size from the fact that a single tree has produced lumber enough to build twenty average-sized, five-room houses. Redwood lumbering operations center in the area between San Francisco and Humboldt Bay, which is virtually the world's only

[3] A board foot is 144 cubic inches of lumber—a piece an inch thick, twelve inches wide and a foot long. Thus a 1 x 12 piece 10 feet long contains 10 board feet; so does a 2 x 3 that is 20 feet long.

source of this valuable timber. Manufactured products include ties, shingles, coffins, cigar boxes, fence posts, grape stakes, siding, flooring, paneling, poles, shakes, and piling. Oddly enough the bark, which is one of the toughest known and is often a foot thick, is of little commercial value.

One of California's most picturesque communities is the town of Scotia, on the Eel River, south of Humboldt Bay. Every building in the town is constructed of redwood, many of them being faced with redwood bark. Muir Woods, Richardson Grove, Van Damme Park—these are but a few of the public forests where countless visitors come to gaze in awe at the gigantic trees.

At length came the day when it was realized that the redwoods were being cut off at an alarming rate, and federal and state authorities, and civic organizations took action to set aside forests as reserves and as government parks. It has been a valiant and at times a bitter fight to preserve the trees for posterity. Although millions of board feet of redwood have been milled, thousands of acres of forest land have been made public domain, quantities of potential lumber remain. Now, of course, it is hauled out by rail or by truck. The Mendocino dog-holes are now deserted except for fishing boats, the wire loading-chutes have rusted away, and the little steam schooner is all but extinct.

But what of her heyday?

2

COASTWISE UNDER SAIL

CONSIDERABLE coastwise traffic preceded the development of the redwood trade. Just before the opening of the nineteenth century, two ships, the packets *Hazard* and *Dispatch,* stood into Boston after a long trading journey to the Sandwich Islands and other Pacific outposts. Among the articles aboard them were exquisite furs from the Pacific Northwest, secured through trading with Indian natives. Boston was soon agog with stories of how these furs were secured by the masters of the two ships, Captain Swift of the *Hazard* and Captain Bowers of the *Dispatch,* all for a few cheap beads or similar trinkets. Promoters hounded the skippers of the two trading ships with proposals to return to this land of fabulous furs and barter in their behalf. And so the year 1801 saw a dozen American ships from Boston doing brisk trading with goods sent out by the Bostonian backers. Take, for example, the cargo of the American ship *Boston*; she arrived at Nootka Sound from Massachusetts by way of England with clothes, blankets, mirrors, beads, razors, sugar, molasses, rum, and muskets, in short, just about everything that Easterners thought would attract the natives and result in profitable fur trading—profitable, that is, to the *Boston's* backers.

The *Boston,* in command of Captain John Salter, arrived in the Northwest territory on March 12, 1803, and immediately started to trade with the natives, who crowded about the ship in canoes loaded down with furs. All went well until, one day, Captain Salter became annoyed at one of the chiefs who had brought back a broken musket and wanted a new one. As a gesture of friendship the redskin also brought a few ducks— records do not state whether the ducks were shot down by arrows or by the new firearm—for the Captain. The chief, bereft even of his broken musket and nursing a few bruises, was kicked off the ship, together with several of his staff. Incensed at such treatment, the natives returned under pretense of resuming trading but soon overpowered the crew; and Captain Salter's head, together with heads of his crew, graced the deck of the *Boston* in a long line, immediately thereafter. Only one crew member escaped, and he had a dented skull. The natives used him to repair their muskets, and it was three long years before this white man escaped on the brig *Lydia,* en route to China.

Promoters in New York and Baltimore got wind of the rich trading done by Boston ships in the Pacific Northwest, and were quick to send more-tactful traders to the area. John Astor of New York City formed the Pacific Fur Company and sent the 300-ton ship *Tonquin,* under command of Captain Johnathan Thorn, to the far Pacific in 1811. On board the *Tonquin* was a knock-down version of a schooner, later called the *Dolly,* ready for assembly and intended for coastwise trading on the Pacific. The *Tonquin* discharged her cargo of supplies and material at what was meant to be a trading post at the mouth of the Columbia, and on June 1 set sail for the northern waters. Putting in at what is now known as Vancouver Island, the crew began trading with the natives. Captain Thorn, like Captain Salter, did not possess the tact and diplomacy needed for trading and soon became embroiled in an argument with the natives, tossing several of the tribesmen overboard. Some of the Indians protested through the medium of tomahawks, and all but five of the crew were killed. Four of the white men escaped to the shore and hid. Several days later the Indians ventured on board the *Tonquin* and were blown sky high by powder planted by the remaining fifth member of the crew. This tragedy to Astor's trading venture was instrumental in bringing about a decision of the firm to sell out to English interests, and Astoria was changed to Fort George. English sovereignty remained over this part of the Pacific Northwest until 1818, when it came under American ownership.

Stories of these Indian atrocities must have reached Europe, for one day the French bark *Morning Star,* under command of Captain Menes, stood into Astoria with a cargo of missionaries from Brest ready to convert the savages to a milder way of living. It might not have been a bad idea if they had sailed direct to certain Yankee ports and had there schooled other masters of packets who brought on trouble with natives by uncivilized methods of trading.

Coastwise shipping was practically unknown in the years prior to 1847. Only two brigs, the American *Henry* and the British *Janet,* carried on any coastwise shipping between the Columbia River and San Francisco, and these went via Honolulu. The discovery of gold in California in 1848 of course set the world on fire, and traffic from every direction headed for San Francisco and the Sacramento River. In 1849, Captain Richard Hoyt, owner of the bark *John W. Cater,* ran between San Francisco, Portland, and Victoria. Another ship that entered coastwise service was the *Sequin,* owned by her master, Captain Norton, who in one round trip between San Francisco and the Columbia River purportedly cleared nearly $20,000.

Farmers of Oregon Territory around Astoria were of course anxious to cash in on the colossal prices of foodstuffs charged the people of San Francisco and the mining regions. Coastwise shipping not being dependable during this period, several of the farmers built and manned the two-masted schooner *Skipanon;* loading her with butter, eggs, bacon, and potatoes, they sailed her to San Francisco and up the Sacramento River. That they would make successful sales was certain; they even sold the ship, and returned on a northbound packet with plenty of gold in their pockets.

During these early days of the Gold Rush lumber was selling at San Francisco for prices up to $500 per thousand, while it was obtainable from the mills along the Columbia for $10 or thereabouts. Owners of the packet *Sylvia de Grasse* loaded her with a half-million feet of lumber secured from Columbia River mills and headed for San Francisco and fortune. Disaster met the ship, however, and she stranded in the Columbia, turning a million-dollar venture into a financial disaster. Several other vessels, however, joined the increasing traffic between San Francisco and the Northwest, including the bark *Success,* owned by her master, Captain William Irving. This same Captain Irving had the good fortune to purchase a large tract of land on which the city of Portland eventually was founded and became a man of great wealth.

Several small schooners enjoyed a novel coastwise trade, operating between Shoalwater Bay and San Francisco, hauling oysters. One of these schooners, the *Loo Choo,* under command of Captain Nelson, in six trips to San Francisco transported over 8,000 baskets of oysters. Other ships in this trade included the schooners *Sea Serpent, Rialto, Columbia,* and *Tarleton.*

The up-cargo from San Francisco was comparatively light, and coasters heading north in lightened condition frequently ran into trouble. The bark *Mindora,* northbound for Portland, lay off the Columbia bar nearly a month before favorable winds gave her an opportunity to cross. After standing into the river she hit a calm and anchored, but a strong current hurled the light ship on the sands and broke her. The bark *I. Merrithew* was lost under similar conditions, as was the oyster ship *Willamette,* which struck Grays Harbor bar. Her crew stayed with the ship because of their inability to launch a small boat, and when rescued were in starving condition.

In 1857 gold was discovered on the Fraser River, and the

demands for passage from San Francisco gave northbound brigs a lucrative business. The brig *Merchantman*, with improvised quarters, carried as many as two hundred passengers each trip and was joined by dozens of other sailing craft. By 1860 ships of all shapes and sizes had ventured into the coastwise trade and were making stops at such California ports as Crescent City, Big River, and Humboldt Bay.

Balch and Webber, mill owners on Puget Sound, had a line of windjammers plying between San Francisco and the North-west, the fleet including the brigs *Cyrus, Cyclops, Rice,* and *Ork.*

Coal from Oregon and Vancouver Island supported such ships as the barks *Amethyst, Vickery, Hall, Leonosa, Scranton,* and *Narramissic.* Lumber ships plying the coast on regular schedules included the barks *Industry, Live Yankee, Sam Merritt,* and *Almatia;* and there were dozens of other offshore ships carry-ing Pacific Northwest lumber to all parts of the world. One ship on regular coastwise service was the *Zenobia,* operated by the Russian-American Ice Company; it was her job to haul ice from Alaska to San Francisco, and she continued in this novel work until 1858, when she struck the San Francisco Bar and was lost.

Coastwise service as it affected San Francisco and the Colum-bia River and Puget Sound by then was firmly established. Sev-eral steamers now entered into coastwise service. These miniature side-wheelers, brought around the Horn in the 1850's, paddled their way to the north, competing with, but not seriously affect-ing, the business of established sailing ships.[1]

All this was in the days prior to the opening of the Mendocino Coast and is, in a way, a story by itself. But these pioneers of the Pacific Northwest founded a coastwise traffic which was a good example for the pioneers of the redwood coast when it came time for them to establish service between San Francisco and the dog-holes of Mendocino.

---

[1] Some excitement prevailed along the Pacific Coast when the Confederate privateer *Shenandoah* raided Pacific waters, burning and sinking some 36 ships. With the end of the Civil War the *Shenandoah* escaped to Lisbon, where the crew were paid off and the master disappeared.

3

A TEAKETTLE GOES TO SEA

F ULL of high resolve and a thinning haze of the bottled
cheer of San Francisco's waterfront, more than one lumber schooner has beaten her way out of the Golden Gate on her
way north, only to run into unfavorable winds[1] and to return
to port pending better weather. Or perhaps she would stand
out on a fair wind and then lie, becalmed, with no sign of a breeze
to take her on her way. Such operational delays were accepted
by the masters of sailing schooners as a part of their job; but
owners—and passengers—were annoyed no end when steamers
such as the *Beaver*[2] or the *Humboldt* steamed past them on an
uninterrupted schedule.

About 1880 some ingenious mariner hitched a steam engine
to one of the little Mendocino windjammers—some say it was the
Beda[3]—and thus revolutionized coastwise lumber transportation.

[1] A strong southeaster tossed many an empty northbound schooner on the rocks,
where the seas made short work of her.

[2] The *Beaver* (1835–1888) was the first steamer on the Pacific Coast.

[3] Authorities differ as to the first sailing schooner to be converted to steam on
the Pacific Coast, and have awarded the honor variously to the *Beda*, the *Surprise*,
the *Laguna*, the *Newport*, and the *Alex Duncan*.

14

No longer were the coastal sailing vessels forced to lie idle, awaiting a wind to take them on their way—and no longer were the small rivers and shallow harbors inaccessible to the lumber-carriers. The ships were made to respond to the will of the pilot rather than to the whim of the elements, for a vessel with a "fair wind in the stoke-hold" can go just about when and where she chooses.

Just the same, it was a sad day for the skipper of the first schooner to be hauled out on the ways for conversion when unsympathetic shipwrights slashed and tore at the quarter-deck, preparing to stow engines and boilers below. They say that the Old Man—a square-jawed, chin-whiskered gentleman of the old school—berated every shipwright who set foot aboard, blasting him for deliberate ruination of a good ship under the pretense of some such tosh as "rapid transportation." Nothing exceeded his scorn for ships of iron—or with machinery in them. Why, what steamer ever could equal the record of the clippers that sailed around the Horn?[4] On top of that he tried to point out to the owners the loss of valuable cargo space through the installation of engines and boilers and the equally valuable deck space lost by deck bunkerage of coal. Perhaps the Old Man had some basis for his arguments—but the conversion went on just the same.

There was little change in the outward appearance of the converted sailing steam schooner. An unorthodox, box-like cabin was built on the afterdeck, and a slim stack rose from this cabin structure just forward of the main mast. But sail was retained, in modified form, and continued to be so for thirty years after the first conversion.[5]

Compound engines of around 100 horsepower, built by the old

[4] The *Flying Cloud* logged a day's run of 433.5 miles while on a voyage from New York to San Francisco—which would be something for even a modern steamer.

[5] When engines were disabled, sails, if they still were carried, got the ship at least into a sheltered cove until repairs could be made. Not so lucky was the *Washington,* however, on a run from Port Blakely, Washington, to San Francisco in October 1906. She ran out of fuel—and Captain Nelson got the crew busy with fire-axes, splitting up a part of her cargo of lumber. It was hard work; but it got her into port in spite of strong headwinds.

Fulton Iron Works of San Francisco, drove a single propeller, pushing the converted ships along at around eight knots if everything went well. Later these grew in size, and the triple-expansion engine replaced the compound. Turbines never came to the steam schooners, which used the up-and-downers until the end of the game.

There came at last the day when a converted vessel was delivered to her owners by shipyard officials and the regular skipper took command. A tug pulled her away from the old Harbor View Shipyard, in what is now the Marina district of San Francisco, got her out into the stream, and left her to her own devices; the hybrid craft now was on her own. Ugly, black clouds of smoke belched from the stovepipe stack and swirled in a choking haze down on the quarter-deck, momentarily hiding the Old Man from view. Coughing and grumbling, he paced the deck, pausing occasionally to look aloft at the now indecently naked masts, whose sails remained furled, and at the hated chimney-pot which continued to spew its murky smoke. Deck hands stood around, feeling helpless; their ship was under way through no effort of their own. Under his feet the Old Man felt his ship vibrating to the hated throb of machinery.

Below deck, the black-gang fed tons of coal to the miniature boiler under the watchful eye of the newly created sea-engineer and his assistant, who was known as the "greaser." The Old Man would have little to do with the black-gang, and they were content to stay below. There was little ceremony when the "monkey-wrench" seamen came aboard; the sailors feared and hated the shoreside aristocrats of steam. Many a broken skull resulted from the fights that flared up when members of the black-gang could no longer stand the slurs cast in their direction by the sailors. But luck was with the advocates of steam on this maiden voyage, and despite their dragging a wheel astern, as the skipper sarcastically called it, the trip was completely without incident. There was even a time when a smile slipped from the skipper's otherwise tight-lipped mouth; that was when they steamed past a sailing ship, lying-to for lack of wind.

16

Bad blood between deck and engine-room hands led operators to alter accommodations, so that the black-gang lived in the port-side of the forecastle and the sailors in the starboard side; it was the same with the deck officers and engineers in the quarter-deck —engineers on the port, deck officers sacked on the starboard side. Mess-hall arrangements called for separate tables; but there were days when feeling ran high and mess gear and foodstuffs littered the air in a gory mess of beans, salt pork, and blood. Today separate quarters are maintained for deck and engine-room departments and, although they can and do get along, the same jealousy prevails.

Coastwise operators watched the performance of the newly created sailing-steam schooner, and their satisfaction was displayed through the conversion orders that swamped the Union Street offices of Charles G. White, and Barnes and Tibbitts of San Francisco and Alameda had more orders than they could handle. Thus followed the conversion of the *Prentiss,* the *Celia,* the *Lakme,* and the *Laguna.* Engine and boiler orders flooded the Fulton, Risdon, and Deacon iron works; and they all turned out small compound engines that were a credit to their craftsmanship.

Then in 1888, Robert Dollar, operator of a mill at Usal, California, ordered a lumber vessel from the yards of Boole & Beaton to be complete with engines. This ship, small and insignificant as it was, only 218 tons, was the first steam schooner to be launched with engines. The *Newsboy,* as this first steam schooner was called, operated between San Francisco and Eureka, hauling cedar logs and a limited number of passengers. Her operation was uneventful, and she finally met her end in a collision with the steam schooner *Wasp,* in April 1906, on Humboldt Bay.

Many of the northern mills built their own steam schooners and towed the hulls to San Francisco, where Fulton installed engines and boilers. The *Helen P. Drew,* built at Hoquiam, Washington, in 1904, was towed to Greenwood, where she was loaded with lumber and towed to San Francisco for completion.

17

The McCormick Lumber Company built ships on the Columbia River and sent them to San Francisco for engines and boilers. The *Klamath* towed her sister ship *Merced* to San Francisco under such circumstances.

Steam schooners that followed the *Newsboy* and were launched with engines were somewhat changed in appearance from the early-day conversion jobs. For one thing, they were some fifty feet longer, and superstructure was added to house officers and passengers above deck instead of below deck as in the sailing ships. Engines were still aft, and the steam schooners were more hybrid than ever, their after section resembling a steamer while the forward end retained the schooner appearance.

The first steam schooner conversions, as well as the first steam schooners that followed, were coal burners, and it wasn't until 1893 that oil for fuel was introduced into the coastwise fleet when the Kerckhoff-Cuzner Company of Los Angeles converted their small steam schooner *Pasadena* from coal to oil burning. An engine manufactured by the Hinkley, Spiers and Hayes Company, developing 190 horsepower, was installed, and received its fuel oil by gravity feed. This change was unsuccessful, and the ship ran but a short time under the new system before it was changed back to coal burning. Later, when pressure oil feed was developed, the *Pasadena* was again converted to burn oil. During the early days of her operation as an oil burner, San Francisco authorities refused to allow her to tie up at the piers for fear of fire; they went so far as to make her douse her fires at the bar and get towed into port.

But oil had been discovered at Petrolia, California, and far-sighted ship operators saw great possibilities in operating ships with domestic oil instead of coal. Ship operators rushed to convert their ships to oil as they had to convert earlier ships from sail to steam; by 1911 less than a dozen coal-burning steam schooners were left in operation.

This change over to oil burning afforded the operators an opportunity to alter their ships. The square schooner stern gave way to a rounded stern, which made maneuvering alongside wharves much easier. At the same time the ships were increased another thirty or forty feet in length. The *Brunswick* was one of the ships altered considerably. Too small for the increased operations of her owners, she was hauled out at Alameda, where she was cut in half and made forty feet longer. This steam schooner, now forty-six years old, is still in operation. The increased length gave the ships a cargo capacity of approximately one million board feet, and they were now capable of sailing anywhere along the Pacific Coast.

Then, in 1905, S. S. Freeman had the *Daisy Mitchell* built at Fairhaven by Hans Bendixsen. This steam schooner was a radical departure from the conventional lumber vessel, for she had her engines amidships, together with her officer and passenger accommodations. The new type ship carried the same amount of cargo, and had an additional loading gear.

Steam-schooner construction skyrocketed in the years 1906–1909, following the disastrous fire in San Francisco, and the entire fleet operated to capacity carrying lumber to rebuild the city torn by earthquake and leveled by flames. Three dozen steam schooners slid down the ways during this time. Then there came a lull in shipbuilding along the coast, with but four ships being built in nearly as many years. It remained dormant until the outbreak of World War I, when the yards were again jammed with ship orders—some eighteen ships were turned out in 1917.

But if the war boom had done well for wooden-ship builders, it also spelled their doom; for steel vessels, infiltrated into the once holy sanctuary of wooden ships, had come to stay. Ship operators, taking advantage of the offer of the United States Shipping Board, junked their faithful wooden wagons in favor of the new steel vessels. It was a simple job to convert the steel ships to carry lumber: the conventional masts were removed, and in their place four masts were installed for operating as many loading gears.

In 1921 only one steam schooner was constructed, the *Quinault,* built for the Hart-Wood Lumber Company. S. S. Freeman built one more wooden ship, the *Daisy Gray,* in January 1923, and is still operating her. A. B. Johnson built the last steam schooner, the *Esther Johnson,* in October 1923, and that spelled finis, so far as wooden steam-schooner construction was concerned. The steel vessels were larger than the wooden ships, a wooden ship being limited in length by the possibility of "hogging." McCormick stretched shipbuilding ideas when he had the *Everett* built—the largest wooden steam schooner to be launched on the Pacific Coast. She was 236 feet long, had a twin screw with two triple expansion engines of 1,400 horsepower, and had a cargo capacity of 1,800,000 board feet of lumber. But her high operating cost did little to encourage other operators to copy her, and she met her doom by fire, off Humboldt Bay, in 1926.

The wooden steam schooner thus had to bow out, replaced by large, steel ships. But she had figured materially in the pioneering of self-propelled vessels and in the historic steps of marine progress from sail to steam and from wood to steel.

4

MENDOCINO DOG-HOLES

THE Mendocino coast is tough and rugged, with mile after mile of cliff-like coastline along its entire length. Aeons of pounding and slashing by the seas have created jagged impressions that look as if the Devil himself had carved them out with a giant axe. Tremendous stands of timber creep down to the edge of the cliffs, and tower over the murky fogbanks.

Mendocino itself is beautiful. There is an elegance and grandeur about the forests and the gardenland of wild flowers that is unmatched. Tall, six-foot ferns seem like blades of grass at the bases of the towering redwood trees. Fertile valleys hidden in the forests, with an occasional glimpse of the ocean beyond, offer picturesque scenery that brings travelers from afar to view this pastoral frontier country. It is difficult to realize that this same country viewed from seaward is not the spectacle of beauty pictured from ashore; to the mariners it is a grim and inhospitable stretch of coast, its only points of refuge tiny "dog-hole" indentations along its rocky stretches.

Nevertheless early-day schooner masters sailed their tiny vessels straight through veils of fog and into these dark canyons, in search of cargo from mills hidden in the deep draws and coves. It took master seamanship to guide a two-masted schooner into such shallow ports, offering little shelter from heavy seas and strong winds. It wasn't as simple as bringing a ship into port and alongside a wharf—for there were no wharves. The schooners tacked into coves where they must lie-to close in—as close to the breakers as safety would permit. Just how close to come was itself a matter of conjecture; and you only had one chance—a single error was fatal.

It was an accomplishment, this laying-to in such close proximity to underwater reefs and ledges with the boiling surf breaking over rocks right alongside. Yet it was done, and done every day of the year, in fair weather or foul, by skippers of the "Scandinavian Navy," of whom more anon. Each day would find some schooner poking her nose into one of the many landings or coves scattered between San Francisco and Humboldt Bay: coves or "ports" bearing such picturesque names as Little River, Russian Gulch, Bear Harbor, Greenwood Cove, and Shelter Cove; landings named for the early settlers, such as Stewart's, Bowen's, Iversen's, and Duncan's. Call them what you wish, they were dog-holes that could be challenged only by the smallest of ships and entered by the most superb of pilots.

Loggers worked the gulches along the coast in the early days, for there was the problem of getting the logs to the mills and no trains ran into the timberlands in those days. Ox-teams pulled the logs from the forests to the improvised landings, usually a distance of not more than a mile, and from there they were transported to mills. Where the mills were situated on a river the logs were dragged to "skid roads," slid down to the river, and rafted to the mill.

A little lumber sea-wagon would stand up the coast to a cove or "port," make its way close-in to the landing—if there was a landing—and moor under the 75-foot cliffs with the help of an anchor or a makeshift buoy. Lumbermen of the port would lower their cargo of railroad ties, shingles, fence posts, tanbark, or piling

Hauling in the spanker-sheet on the schooner *Admiral* in May 1905.

Driving into a rising sea on the schooner *Admiral* in May 1905.

down a wooden slide, called an apron chute, from the top of the cliff to the ship lying under the outboard end. The sliding cargo was controlled at the ship end by means of an "apron," hinged to be raised and thus stop the material when it was just above the deck. A schooner took on its load within two days, the time allotted a ship in an established port; then it went on its way down the coast to San Francisco and the markets.

Later methods employed a wire cable, stretched from the cliffs out into the ocean or cove and anchored. The ship lay underneath the lower end of the cable, and slings of material let down by gravity feed were lowered when just above the deck.[1] This wire-chute method of loading prevailed in such ports as Greenwood, Albion, Little River, Big River, Caspar, Noyo, Hardy Creek, and a dozen others. Franchises were issued to persons building and renting the services of chutes or wire cables; in 1868 chutes such as those in Big River Township were operated by one James Kenney on a 20-year franchise, much as public warehouses and wharves are controlled today.

In 1852 a silk and tea ship from the Orient piled up on the shores of Mendocino, some one hundred fifty land miles north of San Francisco. Members of the crew made their way to San Francisco in the long boat and spread stories of their ship and its cargo. Parties of salvagers were soon on their way up the coast toward Noyo, where the ship supposedly lay on the rocks. Whether or not they brought back any of the rich cargo is of secondary importance; what they did bring to San Francisco were tales of colossal redwood forests that covered the territory for untold miles.

Harry Meiggs, a promoter and operator of San Francisco's famous Meiggs's Wharf, drank in the tales related by the salvage crew. Foreseeing great possibilities in lumbering, as already proved by the mills operating in Bodega forest, Meiggs rounded up a complete set of mill machinery, loaded it on the ship *Ontario,*

---

[1] And before the days of Plimsoll marks on schooners, the tiny vessels took on such heavy loads the deck was under as much as four feet of water, so old-timers claim.

and with an assortment of carpenters conscripted from the ranks of disillusioned miners set sail for the redwood forests.

The *Ontario* made her way up the coast, close in, with—for a wonder—ideal weather in her favor, for clear weather in this particular section, which is usually a region of fogbanks and overcast, is a rarity. They made a landfall in the vicinity of Big River, and entered the little harbor, which is a little more than a cove fed by a good-sized mountain stream. Meiggs was overwhelmed by its splendor; the stories he had heard in San Francisco had failed to do justice to this magnificent gardenland. Stands of giant redwoods made their way down to the river's edge, and the mountain stream seemed like a silver blade cutting its way through the thick timbers. Meiggs, his carpenters, and even the crew of the *Ontario* were greatly impressed with this virgin land. Here Meiggs established his mill,[2] on the bluffs overlooking the ocean, and the settlement of Big River, later to become known as Mendocino City.

Spurred on by Meiggs's success, Captain William A. Richardson, a rich San Franciscan who held large land grants in Mendocino, built a water-powered mill at Albion in 1853, south of Big River, and later another mill at Noyo, near the spot where the silk ship had been stranded. Bands of Indians, irritated by the invasion of their fishing grounds at Noyo, made particular nuisances of themselves in the way of periodic raids, and at length the mill at Noyo was shut down—or burned down by the Indians. Annoyed by this aboriginal horse-play, the United States Army in 1857 established Fort Bragg to cope with the Indian trouble. Albion continued to prosper, and became one of the coast's better-known lumber ports.

Silas Coombs emigrated from Newport, Maine, in 1847 to California and for some time worked around San Francisco, later trying his hand at mining. Soon realizing that mining was not the easy way for him to make a fortune, he headed for Richardson's lumber camps on the Albion River. Being familiar with logging, he soon held contracts for securing logs for the

[2] The California Lumber Company.

Albion mill and for some years worked for Richardson and his successors.

Cutting timber brought Coombs into the Little River country, a cove with a tiny mountain stream making its way out of the forests and into the ocean. He immediately took a liking to this section and staked out property for himself and for his friends. Letters written by Coombs to his friends back in Maine brought out such families as the Reeves', the Sticlneys, the Perkins', and the Moores. They settled around this little forest stream and adopted the name Little River for their settlement; originally the cove had been known as Bell Harbor and later as Kent's Landing, after two original settlers.

In 1863 Coombs, Ruel Stickney, and Tapping Reeves formed a partnership and built a mill on Little River. By this time, schooners were operating between Humboldt Bay and San Francisco, and arrangements were made for them to call at Little River for cargo, as well as at the other ports of Albion, Big River, and Noyo. The first year of operations at Little River saw a fleet of three dozen schooners loading at this port. In 1874 a disastrous fire destroyed the mill at Little River; but within a year a new mill was erected and in operation. This time a small wharf was constructed to augment the two chutes used for loading operations.

Many of the mills and mill towns suffered disastrous fires. Insurance, of course, was obtainable but at premiums so prohibitive that little protection was afforded the coastal inhabitants. When a fire came along, owners fought with what little equipment was available but nearly always lost the battle against the flames. When the fires died down, the rubble was cleared away and the stocky pioneers started to build anew.

Coombs and his friends from Maine knew sailing ships well and set about building schooners of their own when regular coastwise ships passed up their port. By then the volume of down cargo had so increased on Humboldt Bay as well as on the Mendocino coast that ship space was at a premium. Coombs soon settled this problem by turning out the following two- and three-masted schooners at Little River: *Barbara, Hannah Madison,*

Phil Sheridan, Little River, Napa City, Alice Kimball, Silas Coombs, Electra, Brescot, Emma and Louisa, Johanna Brock, Gallatea, and *Mary D. Pomeroy.*

The first mills changed hands rapidly and often. Meiggs lavished such elaborate plans and construction on his mill venture that there was little profit, and after two years he sold out and returned to San Francisco, where he picked up the reins of prosperity and became a man of influence. Some three years later, Richardson also sold out at Albion to the firm of Rawson & Rutherford, who in turn were succeeded by Merritt & Lawrence, then by A. G. Dallas, and later by A. W. McPherson. In 1867 the first Albion mill burned down and McPherson took in a partner by the name of Henry Wetherby when he rebuilt the mill. In the 1890's the Albion mill passed into the hands of Standish & Hickey. Standish, by the way, was a direct descendant of Miles Standish and bore that name. The Southern Pacific Company purchased the mill and properties in the 1900's and operated them until 1929, when the mill was dismantled and the equipment sold. Today Albion is something of a ghost town, with a handful of inhabitants eking out an existence by farming in the area or by running auto camps for visiting vacationers and fishermen.

There was a lot of fun in these venerable Western ports. The two times of the year that are well remembered by inhabitants of the redwood coast are the Fourth of July and Christmas. At those times logging trains pulled into the coastal port terminals, such as Fort Bragg and Albion, from the logging camps with a full load of Finn loggers, ready for their hell-raising two weeks of fun and fight. A practice that was not exactly a credit to the pioneers was that of the saloon keepers when the loggers came to town. The mills paid off in checks from the San Francisco offices, each little more than a piece of paper to a rough and tough Finn, who wanted, not a drink, but a lot of drinks after six months in the woods. Once paid off, the boys would go to the saloons, where their checks were cashed at from five to ten per cent discount, and then they would just stay at the bar and spend their money until it was all gone.

Old-timers pass along the story of Greenwood in the early days when the company owned the only saloon and hotel in town. Here they paid off the loggers in the same manner, by check from the San Francisco office, and here they discounted the checks at the company saloon or hotel, charging five or ten per cent, which is a tidy discount from a $500.00 check, the average logger's pay for six months.[3] Then they accepted the entire business of the loggers, in drinks and quarters. And when the boys had used up all but a few dollars of their hard-earned money they would board the logging train and go back to the woods, to work and await another hell-raising time six months later.

But not all the mill towns were the same. Standish & Hickey at Albion frowned upon saloons in the mill town, and dispensed no liquor on their property. But along came a young fellow, one Bob Mills, who bought a parcel of property across the river from the mill town and made a fortune in a saloon he operated. Discounting, the usual practice here, too, added to his income. There were those who said he bought a barrel of whiskey and sold ten barrels of drinks from it; but then perhaps it had to be cut to that extreme to make it palatable.

Little River, too, is somewhat in the same situation as the other abandoned mill towns. There is no trace of the mill, the wharf and chutes are gone, and most of the population that made up the town has moved away. The cove that once harbored lumber schooners now caters to abalone fishermen. A few old homes remain. Silas Coombs's mansion, turned into an inn by his granddaughter, has been the haven of many celebrities on their fishing trips, including the Governor of California. Trails that at one time felt the hoofs of oxen hauling logs to the mill now feel the pad of fishermen as they beat their way to pools of Little River. Hollywood took over the locality during the filming of *Frenchman's Creek,* a story based on the English coast; their movie-made sailing ship anchored in the cove so long used by schooners of Silas Coombs. Charles Van Damme, a lumber-

---

[3] It is said, and with some authority, that only one payroll was ever sent to Greenwood in the early days, the same money being used over and over again.

man and San Francisco ferryboat operator, purchased the land surrounding Little River, the place of his birth, and upon his death his wife donated it to the state as a park.

Mendocino City, formerly Big River, with a population of less than eight hundred in 1940, is practically a ghost town, in comparison to its former size. The closing of the large mill here in 1931 virtually killed the town. For a while many of the stores and homes were vacant and grass grew unattended in the high, board walks. But recently the town has come to life again through the wartime operation of mills at Caspar and Fort Bragg near by. If Mendocino City has been hard hit, the inhabitants don't let on. Homes in this venerable frontier city stand out as an example of fortitude and deliberate will of the people who live in them. Almost without exception the homes are newly painted, the gardens are clean, even the windows shine. An abandoned fire station exposes two old fire engines with dust and cobwebs covering the once red body, and grass grows on the floor. But as if that is to fool visitors, a new fire engine is harbored in a public garage and any threat of fire to this redwood-built town is speedily handled.

Greenwood, just south of Albion, is another community which has gone the way of all abandoned mill towns, but she has had a roaring good time during the century of her existence. The Greenwood Brothers, William, Boggs, James, and Britt, settled in this area in the late 1840's, and they say it was Britt who led rescuers to find the survivors of the ill-fated Donner Party. Greenwood became prominent in the 1890's when Lorenzo E. White built a large mill here. Prior to that time, White, a Canadian immigrant, had been a bookkeeper for several of the mills.

For forty years the L. E. White mills operated here, White becoming a power along the coast. It was only fourteen hours from Greenwood to San Francisco by steam schooner, and vessels loaded one day could leave at dawn the next morning and be in San Francisco unloading by the same evening. White operated two of the early-day converted sailing-steam schooners, the *Alca-*

traz and the *Alcazar,* and many two-masted schooners. An incline ran from the 150-foot cliffs down to the most easterly of a cluster of three large rocks, from which a wire cable led for loading and discharging. Vessels rode to moorings on the north side of the outermost rock, called Casket Rock. At night the glare from the electric lights was conspicuous at sea, but there have been no electric lights since the mill shut down in 1929.

Greenwood went the same way as all of the lumber towns when the timber was available only at distances, making it unprofitable to ship to the mill and down the coast by steamer. In the 1930's the Greenwood mill was dismantled and the machinery sold. The wire-cable landing and trestle have fallen apart, and the mill has all but disappeared, just a few piles remaining to remind one of a once prominent enterprise. All along the Mendocino coast, most of the old-time ports have similarly declined. The mills are either gone altogether or have gradually disintegrated.

Yet two dog-holes of Mendocino are active today; and if coastwise ports were to be revived these two pioneer ports could resume shipping. They are Fort Bragg, largest town between San Francisco and Humboldt Bay, and Caspar. About the year 1885, C. R. Johnson of Michigan migrated to the Pacific Coast and purchased an interest in the Stewart & Hunter Lumber Company, operating at that time on Ten Mile River, north of Fort Bragg. That same year the company bought timberland adjacent to Fort Bragg and built a mill. Today, after a half-century of continuous operation the Union Lumber Company, as the company is now known, ships millions of board feet of redwood to all markets of the world. This company, one-time operators of the National Steamship Company, has employed such colorful steam schooner skippers as "Hurry-up" Jack Bostrom, "Portwine" John Ellefsen, and "Midnight" Olsen. The brand Noyo, used by this company, was the name of the Chief of the Indians who inhabited the area in the early days. Three of the many ships that comprised the Union Lumber fleet held the name *Noyo.*

Today the Johnson family continues to hold control of the

Union Lumber Company, owning also the Mendocino Lumber Company at Mendocino City. Mr. Otis Johnson, president of the pioneer company, hasn't forgotten that it was largely the steam-schooner fleet that aided materially in the building of the West, furnishing San Francisco and other cities with redwood and pine. For over his desk in a large downtown office in San Francisco hangs a massive picture of the original lumber schooner *Noyo*.

A few of the ports exist on such outdoor activity as fishing. Abalone fishing at Gualala, Greenwood, and Little River is known throughout the Northwest. Even a few stands of redwood still may be found outside of public domain that provide a setting as original as it was when the *Ontario* made her way north. Steam schooners no longer stand into the little ports; and steam-schooner crews no longer meet the lumberjacks of the logging camps at the company saloons for their hell-raising, rip-roaring nights of fun and fight. The remaining company stores have been made into hotels or inns for the convenience of vacationers. Trucks make their way down the coastal highways with lumber cargo that once belonged to sail and steam schooners. The Mendocino coast, so far as coastwise shipping is concerned, vanished along with the steam-schooner era. One old enough to have experienced a night in any of these old-time ports of call or to have sailed on a coastwise steam schooner may not be ashamed of any display of emotion as he stands up the coast and looks in the distance at old-time, landmark cities such as Greenwood, with its white-spired church, prominent from southwestward, or Mendocino City, the city built on the cliffs.

California Lumber Company mill (Harry Meiggs), 1852. Note apron chute,
sliding lumber to lighter below.

Steam schooner *Navarro,* one of the early lumber vessels launched with engines.

Steam schooner *Scotia,* smallest steam schooner built on the Pacific Coast.

Willapa, "double-ender" steam schooner.

"Double-ender" steam schooner *Geo. L. Olson.* Note three loading gears.

"And ye'll never sail again, *Mabel Grey*." The trim three-mast ball header, with a full load of lumber "deck and below hatch," went ashore and broke her back at Redondo Beach, California, December 21, 1905.

5

GRAPE STAKES AND RAFTERS

LUMBER and lumber products were, of course, the principal cargoes of the steam schooners, whose very existence was due to the need for ships of just that type to get forest products from the rugged north coast to San Francisco and other ports as far south as San Diego. Southbound manifests showed such items as dimension lumber, railroad ties, shingles, and tanbark—and many a giant redwood which already was in its prime at the time of the Crusades made the last long journey to some coastal vineyard as a load of grape stakes aboard one of the little wooden freighters. General merchandise for the northbound voyage would be made up of groceries, mill supplies, machinery, and a wide variety of plunder.

The general cargo laden for the trip home to the mills invariably included choice—and not so choice—liquors for the hard-hitting, hard-drinking lumberjacks. For the gentler folk, the little ships carried mail-order goods and various refinements of civilization suitable for snug little homes at the fringes of the forests. It was this form of transportation which brought to the Little River home of Silas Coombs the small organ and the old-fashioned square piano which are still there. Both came out, around the Horn, from Maine in the 1860's. Years later, it was the steam schooner *Daisy Freeman* which loaded up with priceless tapestries, paintings, and medieval statuary and delivered them, safe and sound, to William Randolph Hearst's fabulous estate at San Simeon.

No, the lumbermen were not all of the rough-and-ready sort. Many were men of refinement, lured from their Eastern homes by the stories brought back from California and Oregon. When these chaps got around to it, they married girls from home, and transplanted them to the rugged California coast. It must have been a major feat of adjustment for many of the brides; but most of them stuck by their husbands and played an important part in bringing culture and refinement to the otherwise wild and woolly redwood country.

But some of the Eastern damsels were fastidious, and slightly on the fussy side. They were willing to live in a rough-hewn home, provided they could fix it up with curtains, furniture, fancy rugs, and so on. And they often secured this through the medium of steam-schooner captains. It was not unusual, therefore, to see a member of the Scandinavian Navy shopping around in some swank San Francisco store for curtains, lamps, flower-pots and other "necessities." The skippers didn't relish such chores—but who were they to say no to a millowner's wife or daughter? And such shopping tours could not be delegated to the ship's mess-man or some sailor; they had to be handled by the Old Man himself. It was a happy day for the skippers when the millowners established their own general stores and by special orders through these stores and the mail-order houses obtained the gear required for drawing-room and boudoir. Waterfront legend has it that old Captain Erickson of the *Greenwood,* after one of these early shopping tours, was accosted by waterfront toughs as he made his way back to the ship, loaded down with things which were ob-viously foreign to a merchant skipper. There were two of the plug-uglies and only one of the captain—but he gave them more than they could handle, routing them by blows over the head with what is astonishingly described as an infant's bottle. And then, so the story goes, the doughty mariner's wounds were dressed, on the spot, with bandages fashioned from the contents of another of the packages, to wit, diapers.

Many of the settlers forsook the lumber industry for farming, the lower Mendocino Valley being quite fertile. Apples, prunes, and potatoes[1] were grown in quantities and were shipped, via steam schooner, to San Francisco markets; these seasonal crops produced lucrative cargoes for the ship operators.

Lumber shipments to ports as far south as San Diego permitted, with their discharge, the empty holds to be filled with barley, wheat—and mustard and honey from Hueneme, which then was but an open roadstead, sporting a whitewashed shed on the end of a tiny pier out to just beyond the breaker line. Nor was this the only "outside port" of southern California. There was a shelter of a sort at Port Harford—now Port San Luis— and one at Santa Barbara; but it was pretty much open-sea stuff for such places as Redondo, Port Los Angeles, and Anaheim Landing.[2] Vessels which ventured as far south as Mexico brought back cattle bones—used by the chemical divisions of the sugar refineries in bleaching sugar—as well as deerskin and the inevitable Mexican beans. Southbound cargoes to Mexico included not only mine timbers, but also coal, kerosene, and flour for the mines developed by American capital. Operation of the *Willamette* in the Mexican service, incidentally, brought an interesting example

---

[1] Potato Patch Shoal, just north of the Golden Gate, is named for one of these cargoes, lost when the vessel which carried it hit the coast in a storm. For days after the wreck, literally acres of ocean were covered with floating potatoes. Right then and there it became Potato Patch Shoal—and it is still so listed on the charts.

[2] Calls at the southern California outports were not limited to the lumber ships. In the days of the famous old Pacific Coast Steamship Company, the passenger steamers *Santa Rosa, State of California, Queen,* and the rest called at Redondo, Port Los Angeles, Santa Barbara, and even, in the earlier days, at Hueneme and Port Harford. One by one the southerly "outports" were dropped, the bigger ships making only Los Angeles Harbor in the latter days of the Puget Sound–Portland– San Francisco–San Diego passenger trade.

of what can happen to a name when it crosses a border; the Mexicans pronounced it according to their own rules, and from Ensenada south she was the *"Wee-ya-may-tay."*

The gold rush to Alaska in 1898 offered new fields for the independent brokers who owned their own ships. Fantastic returns were made on voyages to the northland, vessels such as the steam schooner *Luella* being reported as paying for themselves on a single voyage. Passage to Alaska was in demand, and many of the little freighters left San Francisco with such loads of humanity and cargo that they had little or no freeboard. A new territory was being established, and every possible necessity was in demand—foodstuffs, lumber, clothing, and all kinds of supplies. All of this gear was shipped by diverted steam schooners and coastal passenger ships, and as the "necessities" for the mining towns included such things as roulette wheels and dance-hall girls, cargo—and passenger—manifests were interesting. And then there were the great fortunes of gold which were brought back to the states, locked in the ship's strongbox. There is no record of any of these shipments being lost to pirates or robbers en route—the hardened officers of the old coastwise ships saw to it that no one got gay with returning gold.

Among the ships that ventured to Alaskan waters were our old friends *Albion, Corona, Delhi, Tillamook,* ana *Aloha;* the last two carried mail for the government, and it was while engaged in this service that the *Tillamook* piled up on Wood Island, near Kodiak. The *Corona* also got herself into trouble in Alaska, going on the rocks off Lewis Island in 1898. She was refloated but continued in danger of sinking, as the temporary patches did not hold. Suddenly the inrush of water ceased; an investigation revealed that a big blackfish had been sucked into the hole and wedged so tight that fire-axes eventually had to be used to remove it.

Other steam schooners drifted into the coal and fuel business, as the opportunity arose for making a bit more in freight. There were, for instance, the *Unimak* and the *Cleone,* which carried gasoline to Crescent City in the dear, dead days before the underwriters and the steamboat inspectors began to get nasty about tankships with wooden hulls. These two were operated by what was jocularly called the "Bug Steamship Company"—an understandable substitution for the firm's more formal name of Beadle & Antz.[8]

George Fritch, a San Francisco coal dealer, at one time operated several schooners between Coos Bay and San Francisco, hauling coal, and later the steam schooners *Carmel, Empire,* and *Homer* were used in this trade. The Coos Bay coal was used largely for fueling the converted sailing-steam schooners and by inland craft on San Francisco Bay and its tributaries. Better deposits of coal were discovered on Vancouver Island, but large offshore sailing vessels were generally used for this longer haul to markets from San Francisco south.

Another variation from the traditional cargoes of grape stakes, shingles, rafters, and redwood siding appeared in the early days of the *F. A. Kilburn:* she was built in 1902 to haul strawberries and blackberries from a landing near Watsonville to San Francisco. It was about a day's run for a fairly fast ship, and the idea was to beat the railroad tariffs by leaving the southern end of her run in the evening and arriving in San Francisco for the early morning markets. The first year, the long wharf where she loaded Watsonville cargo washed out, and operational losses sent the firm into bankruptcy. Linderman was the receiver, and he placed the "berry-boat" in more profitable service to Eureka.

Rail and truck competition with the steam schooners in the up-trip cargo business has proved fatal to the steam schooners; in this day of speed and percentages, people want things in a hurry, and they want door-to-door service. Good roads, and extended rail service, finally tapped the mill country; and the southbound lumber business was at length limited to Puget Sound, Grays Harbor, the Columbia, Coos Bay, and the Coquille River; when Union Lumber Company sold their last *Noyo,* water-borne

---

[8] Linderman's steamship company also was referred to as the "Bug Line" because of the names of three of his steamers—the *Bee, Wasp,* and *Hornet*—known along the waterfronts as "The Three Stingers."

shipments from Fort Bragg came to an end, and Humboldt Bay became the last lumber-shipping port of any magnitude in California.

But big ships can get into Humboldt Bay, and little by little they crowded their wooden predecessors out of the game. Had it not been for wartime demands, it is likely that the last chapter in the story of the steam schooners already would have been ended. As it is, the ships that hauled lumber for homes and stores, also fence posts and piling and railroad ties and bridge timbers—and forms for the concrete at Boulder Dam—are all but forgotten.

6

BREAKERS AHEAD!

TO THOSE living in the days of direction finders, automatic distress signals, and that war-born wonder, radar, it is difficult to picture the hazards which confronted mariners only a few years ago.

For lack of communication, ships disabled at sea wallowed at the mercy of storms. By day, all they could do was to invert the ensign as a sign of distress; at night they could fire a barrel of pitch on deck, hoping that some passing vessel would see the flames. But there was little likelihood that they would ever be sighted, for it did not take them long to be blown entirely out of the shipping lanes. As the crew took to the long boat and things really began to look tough, a message was placed in a bottle—after the contents had been consumed in a final rite—less by way of summoning help than as a final record of what had happened to ship and crew. Men of the sea in those days were truly men at the mercy of the sea.

A bottle picked up on the south side of the bay at San Diego contained this message, scribbled on a page torn from the log book:

"Off Geronimo Island, December 22, 1877, the ship *James Harford* from Liverpool, bound for San Francisco. Wrecked on the reef south of Geronimo Island 6 miles. Six men lost by up-setting of the starboard quarter-boat. [Names were listed.] Balance of crew trying to make San Francisco. Should we never reach port and this is picked up, please communicate with the British consulate at San Francisco and with Mrs. Elizabeth Haynes. [Signed] William E. Haynes Captain." There is no record that this crew ever reached port safely or were picked up at sea.[1]

Disasters have occurred right in San Francisco's own waters which might have been prevented; at least the survivors would have been aided materially had there been some effective means of communication between ship and shore, or between ships. Vessels overdue at Pacific Coast ports met disaster almost within hailing distance of their port of destination. Often masters of vessels standing into San Francisco reported sighting derelict sailing vessels that might have been saved had there been means of letting those on the mainland know of their difficulty. Early-day news items reveal that the crew of one four-masted schooner, wrecked by a winter storm off the Columbia River, came near starving before they were found by a passing ship. But such incidents on the high seas were not restricted to sailing craft.

For example, take the wreck of the *Hanalei,* a wooden coast-wise steamer of 600 gross tons operating out of San Francisco. On the morning of November 23, 1914, the *Hanalei* was stand-ing down the coast from Eureka with a deckload of lumber, sev-eral head of cattle, some sheep, and a few hogs. She carried a com-plement of 26 officers and crewmen, and she had 34 passengers on board—passengers, even in days as late as this, were secondary to freight.

[1] Incidents of this kind were given a mere mention on the back page of daily papers, indicating that shipwrecks were too numerous to rank as front-page news.

Wreck of *Klamath* at Del Mar Landing.

Klamath after breaking up.

Phyllis stranded at Port Orford, Oregon.

Cottoneva stranded at Port Orford, Oregon.

The ship followed the inshore route.[2] There had been patches of fog and some rain; but shortly before noon the master and mate had a good landfall off Point Reyes, and a course was plotted for the subsequent watches. Captain J. J. Carey, confident that all was in order, left the bridge.

The fog closed in and, although it will never be known, it is presumed that the officer on watch followed the instructions given him. Not long after Captain Carey left the bridge a look-out shouted "Breakers!" and the ship, headed straight for shallow water, went full astern and backed into deep water just in time to avoid being stranded. The master and mate both rushed to the bridge, but the fog had closed in until visibility was zero and a landfall or sighting was impossible. Calculating speed and time, the *Hanalei* was estimated to be in the vicinity of the Golden Gate.

The vessel steamed aimlessly in circles, for what to those on board seemed hours. Anxious eyes peered through the swirling fog for a landfall. Engines were stopped, and all listened, as the ship drifted, hoping to hear a foghorn or the blast of a vessel near by. Several times while they were drifting the pounding surf could be heard, dangerously near; then the vessel would turn into what was thought to be deep water. Why no soundings were ever taken will never be known. From time to time the *Hanalei* sounded her own whistle, both as a warning to other craft and as a call for assistance. They were lost—lost in the treacherous Pacific fog.

And then it happened; the *Hanalei* struck a reef off Duxbury Point, some nine miles north of San Francisco. The whistle alarms sounded by the ship had been heard by employees of the Marconi Wireless Station on Duxbury Point, and through the fog they could just make out the dim silhouette of the stricken ship. Her stern was on a reef, and her bow was in the breakers some 300 yards offshore.

Word of the plight of the *Hanalei* was flashed to San Francisco, and the tugs *Hercules* and *Defiance* were immediately ordered out. Two of Paladini's big fishboats went to assist; and a

[2] Five miles offshore.

Navy transport, the U.S.S. *Rainbow,* was diverted from her course, as was the steamer *Richmond.* Lifeboat crews went out from both the Golden Gate and the Fort Point Life Saving Stations. Captain Curtis, of the Marine Underwriters, organized a relief party with medical personnel, bandages, food, and coffee. A plane was sent by a local newspaper to cover the story of the wreck.

Captain Carey brought all passengers and crew members on deck, and issued life jackets. A Lyle gun was broken out and a line was fired toward shore; but it fell short of the beach and, with its one shot gone, the gun was useless. Two seamen volunteered to take lines ashore, but both were lost in the boiling surf.

The tugs were unable to locate the *Hanalei* and returned to port. The plane also failed to find her and returned to San Francisco. The large craft that had diverted from their courses stood well offshore, afraid that they would meet the same plight as that of the coastwise ship if they ventured too close in. Paladini's boats attempted to run alongside the *Hanalei,* but heavy seas prevented them from furnishing aid. The life-saving crews attempted time and again to run the heavy seas and place a line on board, and stopped only when their boats swamped and they were either lost or swept ashore.

For sixteen hours the *Hanalei* was pounded by the seas; rails, booms, lumber, and hatch-covers began to wash ashore, disclosing that the ship was fast breaking up. Fires built on the beach to illuminate the area lent eeriness to the scene.

In despair, a Lyle gun with 2,000 pounds of gear and nine men was placed on a truck in San Francisco and rushed out to Duxbury, arriving at 1:30 A.M. Several lines fired from the 200-foot cliffs failed to reach the ship; but finally some were placed on rafts carrying personnel, and the remaining survivors were brought to safety.

A final count revealed that twenty-three lives had been lost, exclusive of Coast Guard personnel. Among them were eighteen of the passengers including several women and an infant girl. Captain Carey assumed full responsibility; a board of inquiry suspended his license, but leniency was shown because of the

Captain's heroic efforts to save the crew and passengers of his ship. It was this wreck that hastened the passage of laws requiring radio on board all passenger-carrying vessels; it also brought about the placing of Lyle guns in all Coast Guard stations.

It was on the night of July 20, 1907, that the coastwise passenger ship *Columbia*[8] stood up the California coast bound for Puget Sound ports with some two hundred passengers on board. The sea was calm, but there was no moon and the night was particularly black, with patches of heavy fog prevailing. Captain Peter Moran of the *Columbia* considered navigation so hazardous that he remained on the bridge.

Suddenly off Cape Mendocino, those on the bridge heard a ship's whistle sounding off their starboard bow, and almost immediately a ship's running lights pierced the fog. Captain Moran immediately ordered engines reversed, but as the ship was under way at full speed some precious minutes passed before speed slackened. A series of whistle signals, coupled with desperate moves on the part of both ships failed to prevent a collision and the stranger plowed into the *Columbia*.

The other ship, the steam schooner *San Pedro*, fully laden with a cargo of lumber, cut into the bow of the *Columbia* 30 feet abaft her stem on the starboard side. There was no grinding, no screeching, no tearing of steel; it was a silent, sickening crash that was mortal for the liner. Lifeboats were launched, but owing to the list of the vessel and the huge breach in her bow she sank quickly, and many lives were lost. Captain Moran, true to the custom of the sea, went down with his ship.

Out in the murky darkness lay the little lumber ship. She, too, was hurt and hurt badly—her cutwater was battered, her mainmast broken in two and her forward seams open, letting in generous quantities of sea water. Green water even washed over the deck, she was that low. Amid the flotsam of fence posts and railroad ties that comprised the deckload of the *San Pedro* came survivors of the ill-fated *Columbia*. And with some seventy passengers and crew members of the liner, the *San Pedro* put about

[8] The *Columbia*, built in 1880, was the first steamship with electric lights.

and steamed slowly toward Humboldt Bay. The steamer *George W. Elder,* in the area at the time, also brought survivors to port. At Eureka the entire populace turned out and gave aid to the survivors. Ships passing through the area later searched the wreckage but saw no survivors; and the wreck was logged as one of the coast's worst sea disasters.

Then came the board of investigation and a thorough inquiry into the cause of the collision. A final ruling laid blame on both skippers and upon the mate of the lumber schooner, who lost his license for five years. The master of the *San Pedro* was charged with not being on the bridge during hazardous weather, despite having been called by the watch officer, and the mate was accused of having followed an erratic course. The *Columbia's* skipper also shared the blame for having his vessel under full speed during low visibility.

Fire at sea was another hazard constantly confronting the men of the wooden steamers. Dried out upperworks, oil-soaked bilges, and wooden decks and beams are just the food sought by hungry flames which may arise from an overheated boiler or a capsized lamp. But, surprisingly enough, there was little loss of life as a result of fires in the steam schooners.

Among the fire casualties was the *Sunol,* which lay at anchor in the tiny cove of Little River, California, on the night of October 23, 1900, with her crew making a night of it ashore in one of the company saloons operated by the Coombs & Stickney Lumber Company. A northwest blow came up rather suddenly and the tiny lumber ship strained at her moorings, rolling more and more violently as wind and sea arose. Captain Green, who was aboard, smelled smoke and quickly found that the galley was a mass of flames; a kerosene lamp[4] had been knocked adrift by the pitching of the vessel, and the fire quickly involved the whole superstructure. Captain Green had to jump for it, and was

---

[4] Even in the steam schooners which carried electric lights it was customary, when lying in port, to shut down the dynamo and depend upon oil lights and lanterns for illumination. The brass dining-saloon lamp in the little *Necanicum* would, incidentally, have brought a good price for someone's rumpus room ashore.

severely injured before he got to shore. The fact that the crew was safe in a saloon probably prevented any fatalities, but the little *Sunol* burned to the water's edge and sank.

The steam schooner *Berkeley* left San Pedro in the midnight hours of November 14, 1907, bound for San Francisco. Fire in the engine room was reported by a fireman to the master, Captain A. D. Higgins, who investigated along with the chief engineer and found the waste locker ablaze with a rapidly spreading fire. Before the engine-room gang could get the pumps going and the hoses out, the fire was out of control and the crew were forced to take to the small boats. The steam schooner *Coos Bay* lay-to near by and took survivors on board. Also the *Everett,* largest steam schooner built on the Pacific Coast, was lost by fire off Eureka on October 26, 1926; and the *Berkeley,* but six months old at the time, was a total loss, having burned to the water's edge.

There are many who say that the steam schooner *Daisy* was all that her name implied; she was a conventional little job, but temperamental. One August day in 1926 the *Daisy,* fully loaded, got tired of it all and quietly sank at her berth in China Basin, San Francisco Bay. A day or so later while her owners and crew were wondering what had got into the old girl, she suddenly popped to the surface, little the worse for her dunking. A month later she disgraced herself by plowing through twenty-five feet of an oil wharf at the foot of Mason Street. She went on, playing tricks here and there until—by this time renamed *Redwood*—she managed to get herself on fire off Humboldt Bay and became a total loss, her crew being rescued by the steel steamer *Scotia.* Others lost by fire included *Mary Olson, Wasp, Reindeer, Mukilteo, O. M. Clark, Nome City,* and *Charles Nelson.*

Nearly every time a ship stood in or out of a Pacific Coast "outside" port the skipper and crew took their lives in their own hands. The entrance to Humboldt Bay is strewn with the wreckage of coastwise ships that failed to cross the bar safely, and even San Francisco's own entrance is not without ship loss from the same reason. Heavy seas picked up the small ships and slammed them against rocks or sandbars, breaking their backs and smashing them as if they were but toys.

One of the worst wrecks on a bar was that of the steam schooner *Brooklyn,* which stood out of Humboldt Bay fully loaded with lumber for San Francisco, on the afternoon of November 8, 1931. Heavy seas were running at the time, but Captain Johansen was certain his ship would clear the bar and make her way safely down the coast. Perhaps the skipper was overconfident, or perhaps it was fate that chose this little ship; at any rate she struck the bar so hard her back was broken and she went to pieces on the spot. There was no chance to launch a lifeboat and, even if there had been time, giant seas would have done away with it in short order. Lumber and flotsam from the ship milled around in the heavy seas, and there was no sign of life amidst it. Coast Guardsmen were unable to clear the bar to effect any rescue work, and a Coast Guard plane sent to cover the wreck was unable to make contact because of the fog and the rain squalls.

As soon as the seas quieted sufficiently to allow the operation of small craft, Coast Guardsmen put out, but found no survivors. After several days' search the incident was logged as a major disaster with all hands lost, and hope of finding survivors was given up. Days later, a coastwise ship picked up the second officer of the *Brooklyn* floating on a hatch cover miles from the scene of the wreck, weak from exposure but otherwise little the worse for his experiences.

As the wooden ships aged they slowed up and thus became easier victims of the winter storms. Breakdowns at sea caused severe headaches to both deck and engineer officers and accounted for many ship losses.

The *G. C. Lindauer* broke her crankshaft twenty miles offshore from Cape Blanco on March 21, 1916, while en route to San Francisco from Grays Harbor. The deckload was lost, and water taken on board soon put out the fires. The schooner *Adeline Smith* took the disabled vessel in tow, while engineer officers attempted to effect repairs. They succeeded, but not before Chief Engineer George Ames had suffered severe injuries while working on the engines as the ship rolled in the heavy seas. The *Lindauer* proceeded to port under her own power; but Captain Rohberg was unable to tie up for repairs, as the cargo remaining in the hold was badly needed in San Pedro, and the *Svea* towed her to that port, where the repairs were made.

The *Dirigo,* under command of Captain Davis, had her seams open up during a gale on January 11, 1906, south of Cape Blanco. Fires were put out and the ship rolled helplessly in the troughs. Part of the cargo was jettisoned, and the storm took away the rudder post and rails. After twenty-two hours of distress the steam schooner *Shasta* came across the *Dirigo* and took her in tow for San Francisco.

Deckloads were continually shifting in heavy weather, and many of the little ships stood into San Francisco Bay virtually on their beam ends. The *Chehalis* took on a list while rounding a headland en route from South Bend, Washington, to San Francisco on July 18, 1915. The engine room flooded, and 50,000 board feet of lumber were jettisoned before the ship was righted. Then the ship lay-to, reloaded the lumber, and proceeded south. Later a rip tide nearly capsized the *Esther Johnson* while she was standing into San Francisco during heavy weather; she lost 50,000 feet of her deckload.

The long-standing practice of following the coast close-in was often disastrous. When the *Crescent City* struck Fish Rock she was so close to shore that the gangplank was lowered and passengers and crew walked ashore.

The steam schooner *South Coast,* Captain Stanley Sorenson in command, left Crescent City at noon on September 16, 1930, for Coos Bay with a cargo of 100,000 feet of cedar logs, and was never sighted again. The tank ship *Tejon* reported sighting a floating deckhouse off Port Orford, Oregon, and later the steamer *Lake Benbow* picked a lifeboat and steamed through cedar logs in the vicinity. Wreckage identified as that of the *South Coast* washed ashore, and the vessel is believed to have hit a rock west of Port Orford and to have capsized.

The *Bee,* chartered for one trip to Central America for a

cargo of coffee, on her return trip ran into a full gale. The vessel soon filled with water, swelling her cargo and bursting the decks. The crew made the small boats safely, but the ship capsized. She was finally towed to San Francisco but was never used again, and finally rotted away. Two other ships, the *Wasp* and the *Svea,* capsized and were towed keelside up to port, where they were salvaged.

Collisions were generally due to fog conditions and to the desire of many of the ships to maintain schedules even under such conditions. The *Pomona,* on the afternoon of January 13, 1901, allegedly under full speed, ran down the schooner *Fearless* off Bolinas during a storm, cutting the sailing vessel nearly in half. The *Fearless,* on her maiden voyage, had run into heavy weather; she had lost her deckload and was hove-to, waiting out the storm when run down. She was towed to port and later repaired, while the *Pomona* continued on her way.

The night of February 4, 1921, will long be remembered by coastwise skippers who were unfortunate enough to be on the high seas at the time. From the Aleutians a full gale, which was a credit to that land of eternal tempests, swept down upon the Washington, Oregon, and California coasts. Heavy seas and howling winds played havoc with shipping that night, what with the steam schooner *Raymond* radioing that her engines were disabled and that she required assistance, the *Washington* thirty-six hours overdue, the *South Coast* twenty hours overdue, and the *Oregon* some thirty hours late in making port.

It was on this night that the steam schooner *Klamath,* with nineteen passengers and a complement of thirty-four officers and crew, steamed from San Francisco for Portland, in ballast. Captain Thomas Jamieson, veteran skipper, had checked charts and course and had satisfied himself that Third Mate A. Arneson could carry on the watch alone. A blinding rainstorm lent little visibility, and a twenty-five-knot breeze rolled the lightened ship considerably; but February was recognized as the worst month for weather, and available evidence offered little to indicate that this was other than an average winter night. Arneson carried on

54

with particular caution and diligence. But within two hours the wind increased to a velocity of 75 miles and the ship made little headway. Suddenly the lookout on the bridge yelled a warning of breakers ahead, and almost immediately the ship struck a rock offshore from Del Mar Landing. The skipper and mate made their way to the bridge, realizing the vessel had been blown off her course and on the rocks. Orders were given for full speed astern, but the vessel was beyond the will of the helmsman and they succeeded only in backing her on another rock, damaging the tailshaft and propeller beyond use. Sizing up the situation as hopeless, Captain Jamieson had Wireless Operator Laaetra send an SOS, and all passengers and crew were ordered to the decks.

The steel steamer *Curacao* intercepted the message and advised that she was near by and coming to her assistance with all possible speed. Also the *Everett,* sister ship of the *Klamath* and under command of Captain John Foldat, radioed that she was altering course to seek out the doomed steamer. A seaman, Charles Svenson, took a line ashore and a breeches buoy was rigged up. In the meantime, while transfer of passengers was being made, Coast Guardsmen from Point Arena were on their way, summoned by inhabitants of Del Mar Landing, who had heard the distress blasts of the *Klamath*. A problem of getting an eighteen-month-old baby ashore was solved by an ingenious seaman, who tied a garbage can to his back, placed little Phil Buckley, the youngster, in the can, and rode ashore in the breeches buoy.

The *Everett* and *Curacao* stood by, well offshore, but unable to be of any assistance and without direct communication, as the wireless operator of the *Klamath* had been ordered ashore along with the rest by Captain Jamieson.

In time the gale blew itself out; and there was some hope that the *Klamath,* sitting right side up on the beach, might be saved. But the wind rose again and the staunch wooden vessel, her back already broken by the surge of the breakers, began to go to pieces. For a short time afterward her stern, still intact, stood alone above the breaking seas; the bow—also intact and upright—drifted in behind a rock, and the foreshore was strewn with tanks, splintered timbers, and other wreckage. She was, of course, a total loss; but there had been but one casualty. Snookums, the ship's cat, apparently had taken the "Abandon ship!" order too literally and had gone over the seaward rail.

And then there was the wreck of the German schooner *Bremen,* which, while not involving one of the ships under discussion, is worthy of passing note. It was along in the early 1880's that the *Bremen,* feeling her way in toward San Francisco in the pea-soup fog, struck Southeast Farallon Island. It was fairly calm —for a wonder—and the crew took to the boats. When the fog lifted, the *Bremen* had vanished, having no doubt slipped off the rocks and into deep water. It was not a particularly outstanding wreck except for one thing: the *Bremen* had aboard a full cargo of whiskey, valued even in those days at an astronomical figure. Long and lugubrious were the wails on San Francisco's waterfront. A ship full of whiskey—why, that was practically a week's supply! Forthwith offshore skippers reported sighting fleets of small craft of all sorts, poking around close to Southeast Farallon as if they were all looking for something.

As late as 1929[5] Thomas Patrick Henry Whitelaw, the venerable salvage master, and Bill Reed, a waterfront diver of fame, became interested in the case. Plans were made to salvage the cargo, but nothing ever materialized. Their failure saddened the waterfront all over again but no doubt brought grim satisfaction to those who look upon alcoholic stimulants with a disapproving eye. And off the bleak Farallones, it is said, veteran skippers still lick their lips while passing the grave of the *Bremen.* Perhaps they are visualizing the possibility of a cask of sixty-year-old grog suddenly surfacing and being hauled aboard.

[5] This, you will recall, was during the era in which firewater could not be purchased on the open market; the right people could have made a fortune from the schooner's cargo.

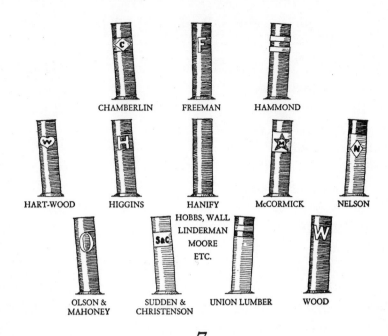

CHAMBERLIN FREEMAN HAMMOND

HART-WOOD HIGGINS HANIFY McCORMICK NELSON

OLSON & MAHONEY SUDDEN & CHRISTENSON UNION LUMBER WOOD

HOBBS, WALL
LINDERMAN
MOORE
ETC.

7

TYCOONS OF THE WOODEN FLEET

THE men who fathered coastwise shipping were, to say the least, a varied lot. There was Andy Mahoney, a former shoe salesman, who won $15,000 in a national lottery and gambled his winnings in a shipping venture. And then there was Charles R. McCormick, who bought a ship he didn't have money to pay for and thereby started on a business career that made him millions. Oliver J. Olson climbed down from a book-keeper's stool to become one of the most successful and influential steam-schooner operators on the Pacific Coast. A. M. "Stove-pipe" Simpson,[1] tiring of paying others to haul his lumber, built his own ship and eventually became the operator of over sixty sailing vessels. Charles Nelson, a master mariner, immigrated from Denmark and ventured into the lumber business, becoming the world's largest shipper of lumber as well as a great millowner and the operator of an important coastwise fleet. Fred Linderman

[1] "Stovepipe" Simpson earned his nickname by his habit of wearing the fashionable stovepipe hat of the era even when out in the logging camps.

57

always wanted to own a ranch and to keep swarms of bees for their honey, which was "Freddie's" weakness; but he got no further than owning a swarm of busy "bugs"—steam schooners bearing such names as *Bee, Cricket, Wasp,* and *Hornet.* Almost without exception, these pioneers started business on the proverbial shoestring and experienced the vexations of too little money but later enjoyed the fruits of their early-day struggles, to become tycoons of the period with enough wealth left over to finance later generations' philanthropic endeavors.

McCormick, operator of a small mill on the Columbia River, walked into the shipyard of Hans Bendixsen, at Fairhaven. On the ways lay a steam schooner, partially completed. The demand for shipping in this year of 1904 warranted speculation by shipbuilders; likewise, the demand for coastwise transportation encouraged the operation of new vessels. McCormick took a look at the little ship, found that the price was $60,000, and forthwith took on option on her. He put down $15,000—which was, incidentally, all the money he had. Bursting with enthusiasm, he rushed back to the San Francisco office to tell his partner, Sydney Hauptman. McCormick quickly found that if there was any enthusiasm running around, it was strictly his own. Hauptman, a bit of a realist, was horrified!

"Charlie," Hauptman said, and his voice must have been something between a croak and a wail, "just what got into you to do a thing like that? You know as well as I do that we haven't got any $60,000—and there isn't a banker crazy enough to lend it to us! Do you know what we are? Well, I'll tell you—we're ruined! Ruined! Oh-h-h!" And he became practically incoherent. McCormick, his enthusiasm still undampened, soothed the feelings and the outraged business sense of his friend and started out to sell stock in his steamship venture.

The option had thirty days to run; but at the end of three weeks McCormick still lacked $5,000 of the contract price. He had shouldered additional responsibilities by contracting for the purchase of an engine for the ship from the Fulton Iron Works of San Francisco. The E. J. Dodge Company was pressing both

Bendixsen and Fulton for the price of the hull and the engine; but, in spite of this, McCormick succeeded in obtaining a five-day extension of the option and finally was successful in floating enough securities to pay for the vessel. She was the *Cascade,* first ship of a fleet of thirty wood and steel vessels, and her purchase was made possible through stock sold to schoolteachers, butchers, grocers, and even the shipwrights who helped to build her. Today the McCormick Steamship Company operates in coastwise, inter-coastal, and world-wide trade, with a fleet of more than thirty steel ships.

The *Cascade* was joined by the wooden steamers *Klamath, Shoshone, Yellowstone, Yosemite, Multnomah, Willamette, Celilo, Ernest H. Meyer, Everett, Wahkeena,* and *Wapama.* All were outfitted to carry passengers; and the McCormick steamers, each with its familiar, star-design funnel marker, became well-known along the West Coast as good ships and "good feeders."

Charles McCormick prospered, his mills building St. Helens, Oregon, from a virtual Columbia River logging camp to a town that boasted several thousand population. He founded the Fir-Tex Corporation, a nationally known wallboard firm; he organized the St. Helens Pulp & Paper Company; and he had retail lumber yards in several coast cities, as well as wholesale yards in San Francisco and San Diego. The McCormick Company even bought out an Eastern firm, the Munson Steamship Company, and operated ships to South America. In addition to the lumber mills at St. Helens it had large creosoting plants for treating piling, which was a lucrative business. During World War I, McCormick built ships for the United States Shipping Board. With offices in New York and San Francisco and in the South Americas, McCormick Enterprises became internationally known.

Today, Charlie McCormick, well along in years and no longer connected with the original company, is not content to be idle. He handles the San Francisco office for young Charles McCormick, who headed for the Columbia River forests as his father had done years before and now operates a good-sized piling and lumber concern. The office is conveniently located, and such old-timers as Freddie Linderman often drop in to pass the time of day and to exchange stories of the days when the old-timers were active on the Redwood Coast.

Oliver J. Olson, son of a Norwegian sailing master, sat on a bookkeeper's stool figuring out profit-and-loss statements for the Wempey Brothers Paper Box Company of San Francisco. But young Oliver's mind wasn't entirely on the figures in front of him; in fact he had made a few figures of his own in the side of the ledger page—figures which had to do with a plan for transporting lumber for the company which employed him. On the way home at night Oliver pondered the question how to get started and what to do and when. He didn't want to sever his connection with the firm, for here was a sure job with security. In order to keep his job and at the same time forge ahead on his own plans, Olson offered a plan to his firm, suggesting that they build a box factory in Oakland, and then he could transport lumber for the new factory in ships that he didn't have now but would get.

The plan worked—partially. The company built the new factory and Olson retained his connection with the company; in fact, they made him manager of the new plant—but nothing was said about transporting lumber. That, however, did not stop Olson; he was determined to have his own ships. It was a fortunate move for the company that they had followed Olson's plan with an East Bay unit; for some ten days after machinery was shipped from San Francisco to Oakland the 1906 earthquake and fire leveled the San Francisco plant.

Captain Olson, Oliver's father, incurred fatal injuries on board ship while crossing the bar into Coos Bay, leaving his widow with eight minor children. Whatever plans young Oliver may have had, and they did include marriage, were altered while he pitched in and contributed toward the support of his family.

About one year later, Oliver saw his way clear to marry and still aid his mother. And now, being married at the ripe old age of twenty-one, he was fired with ambition to get into business for himself. One day he gathered a few of the other employees about

60

him and related his plans for building a ship and hauling lumber from Northwest mills to San Francisco. Partly because of Olson's salesmanship and partly because the plan sounded good, investments were made and the plan was got under way—each investor taking two or three shares for about as many dollars per share. Then a friend of Olson's, one Jim Butler of Nevada, became the angel for the enterprise and furnished the money necessary to complete the construction of the vessel. And so was launched the *Jim Butler,* Olson's first ship; Olson, by the way, owned but one sixty-fourth of it.

The *Jim Butler,* under the able command of Captain Eliason, operated between Puget Sound and San Francisco, carrying lumber to the Wempey Brothers factory in Oakland. The *Thomas L. Wand,* a second steam schooner, secured in the same manner as the *Jim Butler,* joined in coastwise service. Olson was now a full-fledged ship operator on this route.

Business boomed after the 1906 holocaust in San Francisco, and new ships were needed. At about this time Andrew F. Mahoney, a shoe salesman, won the Louisiana lottery grand prize of $15,000 and wanted to invest it. He looked about, and friends told him of their returns from the Olson steamship stocks. Andy Mahoney hotfooted it to Olson, laid the entire $15,000 on the desk of the shipping executive, and right then and there started the Olson & Mahoney firm.

It was a prosperous but stormy partnership. Each partner was a supersalesman and was headstrong. Frankly, they didn't get along together; and minor incidents—humorous to others—embroiled the two serious, hard-shelled businessmen. There was, for instance, the time Mahoney took it on himself as partner to have the hulls of the Olson & Mahoney ships painted green. Now green to an Irishman is beauty in itself; perhaps it reminded Mahoney of the hills of Erin. But to a waterfront accustomed to conventional colors such as white superstructure and dark gray or black hull—well, green just didn't fit in. Olson was well steamed up when he heard about the decoration job on the ships. He stormed into the office, but just before reaching Andy's quarter-deck, he turned on his heels and walked out. Olson sought out the port captain of the company and directed him to paint the largest white "O" possible on the stack of each ship painted green! That was how the stack design of the Olson & Mahoney line came about.

The Olson & Mahoney stock was once so popular that when a new issue was released for the building of a new steel ship so much stock was sold that there were no shares left for the owners. They had to be content with lending their names to the ship— it was the *Olson & Mahoney*.

Many interesting incidents came up in the everyday operation of the Olson firm, just as they did in all coastwise operations. For instance, in 1922 Olson sold the steam schooner *Virginia Olson* to the E. K. Wood Lumber Company. The sale was completed while the vessel was alongside the dock in San Pedro; now the ship while alongside was considered Olson's property and away from the pier ownership of it reverted to its purchasers. Some ten minutes after the *Virginia Olson* got under way and moved out into the stream she was sunk in collision with the steam schooner *Claremont!*

Captain Clark, a long-time associate of the two shipping men, came to their offices one day and laid before them a plan for operating a ferryboat between San Rafael and Richmond on San Francisco Bay. The two men saw the possibilities of such a business and called in their friend, Charles Van Damme, to assist in financing the project. Today this company is still in operation with Andy, Jr., and Oliver, Jr., as executive officers.

But the temperaments of the two shipping men, Olson and Mahoney, were either too different or too much alike, and there came about a dissolving of the partnership in 1916, with Olson purchasing the floating stock. Both retained their equities in the Richmond–San Rafael Ferry and Transportation Company. Mahoney attempted to re-enter the coastwise field but this business was at a lull in the after years, and he retired. In 1936 Andrew Mahoney passed on, and despite the open secret of hard feelings between the two men, those near to Olson say that he

Mary Olson after fire in Cuban waters. This
wreckage sold for $35,000.

Temple E. Dorr limping into port after collision at sea.

Tanker *Frank H. Buck* on rocks at Monterey. This vessel was pulled off by ex-steam-schooner salvage ship *Homer*.

wished old "Andy" were around again—yes, he could paint the ships—even the ferries—green.

Oliver J. Olson continued to prosper and became an influential man in San Francisco financial circles. He was chairman of the board of a nationally known oil company; he played a part in financing the shipping ventures of a former Governor of California, "Sunny Jim" Rolph, and was the director of a bank and several large corporations. Olson lived long enough to realize the dream of installing his wife and family in a virtual castle situated at Sea Cliff, San Francisco, overlooking the Golden Gate. He did well by his children, affording them college educations and for the boys a place in his business world, all this with the limited education of a single year in high school.

George L. and Whitney Olson followed in their father's footsteps and entered the steamship business. They didn't always proceed in the manner of old Oliver; he couldn't quite see the business of handling obstinate skippers with kid gloves. There were times when he questioned their methods and found it appropriate to use sea language that the old mariners seemed to understand; but he gave way for the more cultured method when he saw it brought the same results. And before passing away in 1940, Olson saw his boys capably operating a fleet of steel vessels in intercoastal trade. Today, only one wooden vessel is operated by the Olson company, the *Whitney Olson* until recently under the command of Captain "Caspar Charlie" Carlson.[2] The old *Whitney Olson* still rides the breakers along the coast between Coos Bay and San Francisco as she has done for so many years.

Captain Charles Nelson, a native of Denmark, came to the Pacific Coast in the early 1870's and operated sailing craft between San Francisco and Humboldt Bay. He invested in a mill on Humboldt Bay and soon saw it expand greatly. Along with the expansion of the mill came the expansion of the ships for hauling lumber cargo. Captain Nelson retained a hand in the

[2] Waterfront gossip has it that Caspar Charlie is now master of a large offshore vessel engaged in war operations in the South Pacific, and has recently made a name for himself by unloading his ship in the fastest time recorded during this war.

ship operation and sent to Denmark for his nephews, George, Robert, and James Tyson. Robert was brought into the company and groomed for the managership, with the old skipper handling all the ship operation. Mills were added to the firm's enterprises at Coos Bay, at Grays Harbor, and on Puget Sound. Nelson soon became known as the world's largest shipper of lumber.

Passenger liners were added to the fleet of Nelson ships. The Spanish-American War called for transports, and the federal government requisitioned the Nelson passenger ship *Charles Nelson*. She was converted to carry troops 'tween decks, and made several trips to the Philippines. In 1910 this old-timer caught fire on Humboldt Bay and burned out her engine room, but the engines were salvaged and went into the Nelson ship *Mukilteo*. Then the ex-*Charles Nelson* was rebuilt as a lumber barge with special loading gear on board, operating for years until she finally wound up on the San Pablo Bay mudflats.

At the time of Captain Nelson's death, the Nelson Steamship Company and the Nelson Lumber Company were among the wealthiest and most powerful on the coast. Perhaps its great size was what caused the company to topple over, for when hard times came along the Nelson people had a tremendous fleet in idleness —tied up with burdensome insurance, maintenance costs, and wharfage fees. In the early 1930's the company went into receivership, an example of the uncertainties of the lumber and shipping business.

The days of amassing wealth overnight are not gone, but they certainly are not as plentiful, especially in the steamship business. There were days when Freddie Linderman and Oliver Olson were in New York during World War I—Olson with $300,000 in his pockets from a ship sale, wanting to spend it on some new ship or new venture, and conservative Freddie trying to keep him from spending it all right away. The old coast has lost most of these early tycoons, and along with them have gone their methods for advancement, but they will never be forgotten as the founders of the West and as pioneers of shipping and lumber companies that today lend prominence to the Pacific Coast.

8

FROM *SHINGLES* TO GARBAGE

GENERALLY speaking, when ships become obsolete and are replaced by newer and larger ones, the tired old veterans are towed to obscure waterways and are left to relax and stretch their planks to their hearts' content. But not so the steam schooner. As one operator lays up one of these ships, another operator comes along and recruits the old packet for new and often varied service.

Steam schooners have been employed in capacities far beyond the conventional operations of hauling lumber and lumber products; they have been converted to cattle-and-reindeer carriers, fish-reduction ships, garbage ships, dredges, wrecking-and-salvage ships, gambling barges, gasoline and oil tank carriers, and even gunboats. Its open deck with its engines aft, together with its shallow draft, have made the steam-schooner design popular in these diversified fields.

In 1911 the city of Oakland was confronted with the problem of disposal of refuse. Owing to rapid municipal expansion and the position of adjacent cities, shoreside disposal through the establishment of dumps was not practicable. The solution lay in hauling the garbage to sea and tossing it over the side. Bids were called for, and Fred Linderman, a veteran steam-schooner operator of San Francisco, was the successful bidder for the job of getting rid of Oakland's fragrant waste matter.

Linderman looked over the field of available steam schooners and finally purchased the *Signal* and the *Aberdeen*. The old vessels were altered to carry bulk loads of garbage, and a plan was developed for sending the ships to sea alternately, each three times a week, to dump their loads some twenty-five miles outside the Golden Gate. This procedure ran along smoothly until 1913, when the *Signal* foundered off San Francisco heads during a storm, with the loss of several of the crew.

In January 1916, the *Aberdeen* struck the bar while standing into San Francisco Bay and was lost, with casualties, including her master, Captain Peter Knudsen. Oakland authorities then built giant incinerators and disposed of garbage by burning.

After several years Oakland again exhausted its ability to cope thus with the increasing refuse problem and once more turned to the sea for a satisfactory solution. Linderman was again the successful bidder, and this time the steam schooners *Tahoe* and *Hoquiam,* altered by the installation of ten bunkers on the deck of each ship, were employed for the job. The method of disposal at sea was by gravity feed, the refuse sliding down the raised bunker bottoms with the motion of the swells as the garbage ships lay-to; hydraulic sprays were installed to facilitate unloading if the gravity method was too slow in a calm sea. Dumping took from a few minutes in lively water to as long as ten hours if the seas were calm. The ships carried a capacity load of 600 tons each, at the contract price of 85 cents per ton. A complement of twelve officers and men comprised the crew, taking one ship out one day while the other was being loaded, the second ship the next while the first loaded.

Linderman had a difficult time recruiting officers and men for the job of hauling garbage on steam schooners. Notwithstanding the fact that they would be at home with their families each night, the berths were not too attractive. It is not difficult to understand why.

"Freddie, vy don' you giff oop diss idea? My vife, she say I got to stay on de ship if ve go on hauling svill. She say I shtink —und, py Yesus, she iss right! Giff it oop, Freddie! Let's haul shingles, und not garbage!" Such were the complaints of masters who had been with Linderman for years and years. However, they would have followed "Freddie"—as everyone called Linderman—to the ends of the earth if that had been possible in a steam schooner.

A long series of complaints from coastal cities, to the effect that their beaches were being strewn with Oakland's garbage, led to the appointment of an inspector to accompany the "salad barges" on each trip. It was his sole job to decide just where the garbage should be dumped in order that coastal communities might not scream about the grapefruit skins, melon rinds, and other unpleasant things on their beaches. The inspectors would get a fix on the ship's position when off the Farallones, and then, figuring so many minutes' run on a given course to a "safe" dumping area, would stand there, watch in hand, until the proper time had elapsed. More than once facetious engineers would slow down the engines, thereby throwing the inspectors' calculations off by several miles and bringing new complaints as the refuse drifted up on occupied beaches. In 1931 Linderman sold the *Tahoe* and the *Hoquiam* to the scavenger company which held the Oakland garbage contract; the company ran them until 1943, when both were reconverted as cargo carriers and sold to foreign registry.

Five other steam schooners—*Iaqua, Pasadena, Homer, Greenwood,* and *Chehalis*—were converted into salvage steamers, and were responsible for the recovery of many thousands of dollars' worth of cargo and gear from stranded ships. It was in 1915 that the *Iaqua,* then employed as a wrecking ship for the Union Iron Works of San Francisco, was sent down to Cedros Island, Mexico, where she helped salvage 9,000 tons of cargo and gear from the wrecked Dutch motorship *Malakka.* The motorship had hit the rocks near the north end of Cedros on the night of December 18, 1914, almost at the same time that the American-Hawaiian steamer *Isthmian* had gone ashore on the south end; in each case, magnetic disturbances incidental to a storm were blamed. The bones of the *Malakka* were visible for many years afterward, but the *Isthmian* got off and reached San Diego, her forefoot rolled up under her and her No. 1 hold full of water.

It was in August of the same year that the *Chehalis* stood out through the Golden Gate, bound for Papeete Harbor, fully equipped as a salvage ship and with a crew of expert salvage men on board; Captain Stousland was in command. The *Chehalis* had been chartered by two San Francisco lumbermen—Christensen and Hooper, who had purchased the wreck of the German steamer *Walkure,* at Papeete, for $29,000, on a "where-is, as-is" basis. It was no easy job; but Captain Stousland was equal to it, and after building coffer dams and doing other extensive work, he brought the *Walkure* to the surface late in March 1916.[1] The salvaged ship was towed to Hawaii, where she was reconditioned for the trip to San Francisco. She was renamed *Republic* and was granted American registry; a full cargo was rounded up for her in Hawaii, and she went on from there to San Francisco under her own steam. Captain Stousland, a practical soul, also succeeded in filling the *Chehalis* with a capacity load of copra for the homeward voyage. The owners then gave him a well-earned vacation, which included the use of an automobile—a luxury in itself in

[1] This was, of course, during World War I, when ships were so scarce that anything capable of salvage was worth money and lots of it. Rotten Row gave up many of its dead ships, and the big German freighter, *Sesostris,* which had lain on a Central American beach for thirteen years, was hauled off and fixed up for sea once more. The late James Rolph's resurrected three-masted ship *Golden Gate* is reported to have paid for herself on her first voyage.

those days. The *Republic* was placed on the market; but early offers were not satisfactory to her new owners, who were in no immediate need of cash and who could use her profitably in their own lumber operations. Finally she was sold for $1,200,000, the profit on the job having been approximately a cool million.

The *Homer,* one of the few twin-screw steam schooners, was operated for a time by the Pacific Steamship Company, and then was sold to the Merrit-Chapman & Scott salvage firm, who used her in various jobs of maritime reclamation. The *Pasadena* was sold in 1929 by the Albion Lumber Company to the Haviside Company, the big San Francisco rigging and salvage firm, which refitted her with salvage booms and other heavy gear and used her as a tender for their derrick barges. Later she operated between San Francisco and San Pedro as an "oil-skinner," pumping oil out of bilges or off the surface of the water, where it had been spilled in loading or discharge operations—she was equipped with separators for reclaiming the oil. Later, it is said, she got a job as a seagoing tug, being sent down to Central America to tow home a four-masted windjammer.

The steam schooner *Fair Oaks,* rigged with clam-shell buckets, was used to clear the north channel into San Francisco of a rock formation. Working all through the winter months of 1914, she did a thorough job; it may not have been spectacular but was important for coastwise shipping. Another steam schooner which was converted into a dredge was the *South Bay,* which was rigged as a seagoing hopper-dredge and whose operations included the first serious work at creating a deep-water channel across the bar at San Diego away back in 1911.

Cattle hauling, between the islands of the Hawaiian group, took the *Cascade,* the *Sierra,* and the *Shoshone* in their final years, while, far to the north, the *Bee* was engaged in an activity somewhat similar but with one important exception—the *Bee* was in Alaska, and they had her hauling reindeer. Later the *Bee* came back to the lumber game and was wrecked off Salinas Cruz, Mexico; they towed her hulk back to San Francisco, but she was never used again.

71

Several West Coast fish-reduction outfits bought steam schooners to serve as tenders and mother-ships for sardine and whaling boats, or as floating reduction plants—a reduction plant being an assortment of retorts and other gear which, by the use of heat, turn edible or nonedible sea life into fertilizer and a smell which can be detected several miles to leeward. This sorry fate befell, among others, the *Bertie M. Hanlon,* the *Centralia,* the *Willamette,* the *F. S. Loop,* the *Prosper,* and the *Martha Buehner.* The *Loop,* her boilers little more than a beautiful memory, was equipped in her old age with an elaborate set of reduction gears and—of all things—a Liberty motor salvaged from the air force of World War I. It actually made her go; but the fuel bill was appalling, and they finally sent her down to Central America under her aging square foresail—set from one of her own cargo booms—and a square main obligingly loaned by the four-masted schooner *Lottie Bennett.* Thus you might call her, for want of a better term, a brig. It was an outlandish getup; but it took her to her destination and, her skipper swore, it got her back. Incidentally, the veteran steamer was engaged in the production of canned dog-food at the time.

A gambling syndicate got the *Johan Paulson,* and operated her as a gaming-barge just outside the three-mile limit in southern California, until legal authorities went through their books and found a way to spoil the scheme. The *Empire,* after a long career in the lumber game, was sold to a Central American republic and became a gunboat; and the *Cleone* and the *South Coast,* with tanks built on their decks, operated as gasoline-carriers between San Francisco and Crescent City; both were lost during heavy winter storms.

Ambitious "special service" operators continue to comb the mudflats with a view to recruiting steam schooners for other work. Some, being essentially feminine, hide their age under added coats of paint; then, when their new operators put them into service, heavy weather opens their seams and they founder. Other old ships have engines which no longer can stand the strain; crippled, they are towed to the mudflats, to remain until they rot

Breeches-buoy rescue.

Passengers riding wire loading cable from schooner *Irene* to shore.

Mary Olson under construction at Humboldt Bay.

Building of three-masted schooner *Sotoyome*
on the Albion River.

O. M. Clark under construction
at Aberdeen, Washington.

Launching of the three-masted schooner *Sotoyome* on the Albion River.

away. There are few steam schooners in operation today; with the end of hostilities these few are sure to be replaced by newer, larger ships. And with them will pass the last ties with early Pacific Coast steam navigation, along with the mills which have ceased operations, the few operators who may remain, and the original "Scandinavian Navy" who, like their commands, are fast becoming "Finished with Engines."

9

MASTER CRAFTSMEN

SHIPYARDS of today are like the yards which turned out the steam schooners in one respect: both built ships. And there the similarity ends. The regimented bedlam of the modern yard bears no more similarity to the relative calm and quiet of the old-time plant than a clipper ship does to a transoceanic plane.

Perhaps it is the difference in materials. Your old shipwright worked in wood, hewing out timbers and planks from trees which had taken a long time to grow in the peaceful solitude of the coastal forests. Today you are working in steel, and bending it to your will requires the staccato roar of the riveter, the sputtering torches of the welder and burner, and the hum of hundreds of different kinds of power tools. The quiet of the wooden shipyard was broken only by the occasional buzz of a steam-driven saw, the liquid "cheep, cheep, cheep, cheep!" of the caulking-mallet, and the measured strokes of the maul, as long drift-bolts and spikes were driven home.

There weren't many engaged in the enterprise, at that; it was a mere handful of men who were responsible for creating the fleet of more than two hundred wooden steam schooners that plied the redwood coast, carrying lumber to San Francisco and the ports farther south. With only the most meager of tools they constructed hulls in the back waters of San Francisco Bay or Humboldt Bay—or they would journey to the mills along the Mendocino shore and contract to build a ship on the spot. It was these latter jobs of frontier shipbuilding which gave rise to the old saying—"They parted the forests, and out rolled a steam schooner."

Many of these early shipwrights were men who ran away from hungry foreign ships[1] or who had been lured to the West by tales of easily found gold. They soon found that riches did not grow on trees and that even with the privation and hard work of gold mining it was pretty much of a chance. Consequently, one by one they deserted the mines and picked up their old professions. There were, of course, ships' carpenters among them, and it was largely the pioneering courage—and technical skill—of these frontier craftsmen which gave California and the rest of the coast her early-day shipbuilders.

An outstanding California shipwright was Hans D. Bendixsen, a Dane, who had learned his trade in Copenhagen and Aalborg. He shipped out as carpenter in a sailing vessel bound for South America, and finally worked his way up to the Pacific Coast, where he decided to quit the sea. For several years he worked in the San Francisco yard of Matthew Turner—whose beautiful little brigantines are still tenderly recalled by old-timers—and then moved to Eureka. There, in 1865, he went into partnership with a shipwright named McDonald, turning out a sailing vessel called the *Fairy Queen*. Later he took his brother into business as a partner and finally he branched out for himself at Fairhaven, on Humboldt Bay. In the thirty-three years in which he was in business Bendixsen built no less than 113 wooden vessels, of which seventeen were steam schooners.

[1] Many of California's most stalwart citizens came to this country by the simple process of running away from some "hard-case" windjammer; in those days all that they would have to do from then on would be to pay their alien head-tax and apply for citizenship.

It was no easy road to fortune. More than once, Bendixsen and his backers were thrown into grim financial difficulty as a result of operational losses of vessels which they had financed. And on one occasion the entire yard was destroyed by fire. But he kept on until about 1900, when he sold the yard for $250,000 and retired; he passed away two years later. For several years J. H. Price, of Bandon, Oregon, ran the old Bendixsen yard; then he sold out to McCormick and moved to St. Helens, Oregon. Except for a few repair jobs by William McDade and other local shipwrights, Fairhaven passed out of existence. During World War I, the late James Rolph—long mayor of San Francisco and later governor of California—bought the old location, and started building wooden vessels for government contract. Most of these vessels were barkentines—four-masters and five-masters—and while their lines definitely were not those of a clipper ship they were able vessels with a fine carrying capacity, and they did the work for which they were designed. The genial mayor changed the name of the settlement from Fairhaven to Rolph. After the war things quieted down, and Rolph became about as much of a ghost town as Fairhaven had been when he bought it.

William A. Boole, a San Francisco shipwright, established a yard at Oakland in the middle 1880's, building many sailing vessels; among them was the schooner *Prentiss,* later converted to steam. Boole's brother, George W., did business in the 1870's as "Boole & Webster, Shipwrights, Calkers, and Sparmakers"; and there was a further variant of the family's business name, the shipbuilding firm of Middlemas & Boole. In 1909 the Boole interests sold out to Moore & Scott, and today what started as a somewhat insignificant launching-ways is a yard covering forty acres of land and employing thousands of men. George Boole, whose contributions to the steam-schooner fleet included the *Point Arena* and the *Westport,* died in 1908.

The name Dickie is one which has been well known in coastal shipping and construction circles for many years; the firm originally consisted of John, James, William, and George Dickie, who in 1875 had offices at 642 Second Street, San Francisco, and a shipyard at Hunter's Point. In 1882, the Dickies learned—the hard way—that foreign entanglements may prove expensive. It seems that they took on a repair job, on a foreign gunboat, and she was docked for a long time, the repairs being of an extensive nature. Any hints at settlement as the work progressed were brushed aside, and there are quaint little tales to the effect that the money intended for the job was actually expended on what was definitely a More Abundant Life for the representative of the foreign government. To be blunt, he invested it in wine, women, and song. Then came the day when the job was done —but before payment could be made there had to be what are termed sea trials. It's an old trick, and the surprising thing is that the Dickies fell for it. Anyhow, she headed out through the Golden Gate on her alleged trial run—and that was the last that San Francisco saw either of her or of the foreign agent. That sent the firm into bankruptcy; but two of the brothers, John and James, salvaged what they could and opened up shop again, this time at 7 Spear Street. Later John Dickie bought the old Hay & Wright yard at Alameda and turned out, from that and other coastal plants, several steam schooners. Ships from the Dickie's San Francisco yards included the steam schooners *Arcata, Newport, Newberg,* and *Samoa;* they built the *Acme,* the *Centralia,* the *Gualala,* and the *Vanguard* in Alameda, the *Del Norte* in Tiburon, and the *Doris* and the *Willapa* in Raymond, Washington.

There were several other San Francisco area yards as well— W. F. Stone, Hay & Wright, and Charles G. White—all of which turned out wooden vessels but about whose activities little record remains. Other shipwrights—such as Peterson, who built ships along the Albion River—today are virtually unknown. Even John Lindstrom, who built more steam schooners than any other man, died in virtual obscurity, and not even the Chamber of Commerce of his home town of Aberdeen, Washington, can supply the firm's early history. Only three of the old yards which went in for steam schooners—Kruse & Banks, and Matthews Shipbuilding Company, both in Oregon, and Moore Shipbuilding Co. (Boole)—remain in existence today.

10

STATEROOMS BUILT FOR THREE

FOR many years the one means of access to the dog-holes of Mendocino was via steam schooner, and many of the lumber ships that regularly plied the coastal water between San Francisco and Humboldt Bay were fitted to carry passengers. Considering the limited space, most of the cabins were comfortable, but there were a few vessels—despite their owners' boasts of "fine accommodations"—in which the staterooms were of the order of rope lockers with white paint smeared over the bulkheads.

Competition was keen among the ticket agents of San Francisco, and the solicitors would go to great lengths—often taking liberties with the facts—to sell passenger accommodations on the coastwise ships. Hotel clerks, too, were paid from fifty cents to a dollar for every passenger sent to the agent offering the cut. Many prospective passengers, journeying by steam schooner for the first time, wanted to see a photograph of the vessel in which they contemplated sailing. The ticket agent, with a great sweep of his arm, would point to a picture of an Atlantic liner gracing the wall of the office: "Madam, the vessel on which you are about to sail to Greenwood is exactly like this photograph—only the local ship doesn't have a piano." The agent would then go on to explain why a piano wasn't necessary for a trip consuming little more than fifteen hours. The next morning would find the passenger, ticket in hand and with luggage piled high, down at the pier awaiting the docking of the northbound "liner." One may imagine the disappointment that was in store when an insignificant lumber schooner poked her nose around the pier-head to pick up the two or three local passengers bound for the north. Most of the passengers, disgruntled though they must have been, sailed on the piano-sized "liner," and because so few took the trouble to come back and register complaints the ticket agents continued to "impress" prospective passengers with the back-wall liner speil.

Early-day steamship business was conducted along lines appropriate to the times, and was largely unorthodox; it was based mainly on the law of supply and demand. If accommodations were readily available, the silver-tongued ticket agents would extoll the virtues of their coastwise packets beyond the realm of ordinary imagination; if times were good and there happened to be a demand for passenger space, the same agents would assume a take-it-or-leave-it attitude, at the same time skyrocketing prices and catering to those persons offering the highest price for the accommodation. Few tariffs—if any—were filed with governing agencies, and the passenger in those days seldom knew if he was to travel virtually at the expense of the steamship company —if a rate war was on—or if he would have to pay an excessive price for his ticket.

Once on board the northbound ship, the disillusioned passenger would be guided by a seaman to a dingy stateroom with three-high-bunk accommodations. Adding insult to injury, likely as not the passenger would find himself assigned the top bunk, often called the "Aunt Mary." There are several explanations why the third bunk of steam-schooner cabins has been termed "Aunt Mary." One of them derives from the converted sailing-steam schooner *Arcata*. One day, so the story goes, a spry, white-haired old lady, bag in hand, boarded one of the lumber ships as it lay alongside the dock in San Francisco.

"Are you the Master?" she asked an officer on deck.

"Yes, mum," replied the grizzled mariner, removing his weather-beaten cap.

"I'm Mary Jackson of San Francisco. I want to visit my niece at Albion, and they say on the dock your ship is going there. I want passage, if you please."

The puzzled skipper nervously fumbled his cap in hand.

"Diss iss a lumber wessel, not a passenger ship," he said. "Ve don't take passengers; ve never haff taken passengers."

"Doesn't make any difference, my man—not a bit of difference. My niece married some upstart millman near Albion, and I haven't heard from her. I want to see if she is all right. You are going there—the dockman said so—and so am I."

With that the determined old lady pressed some gold coins into the hand of the perplexed skipper. The skipper and the mate cleared out of their cabin, giving it to the woman passenger; and the little old lady slept in one of the three-high bunks, thus originating the third-bunk name—Aunt Mary. Similar desires of other Aunt Marys to see their frontier relatives, and desires of relatives to visit their Aunt Marys, created the steam-schooner passenger business between the many ports of call along the Mendocino coast and San Francisco.

Three-bunk staterooms were the natural thing for passengers, because such rooms were conventional for officers of the sailing and steam schooners operating along the coast. Space was definitely at a premium, all that could be spared being given to cargo. When the decision was made to cater to passenger transportation, the three-high-bunk-stateroom idea was applied to passenger space. Owners or operators cared little if a third passenger was thrown in with a honeymooning couple; in fact, this presence of a third person in a cabin often created embarrassing situations

(*Top*) Steam schooner *Acme*, Eureka–San Francisco lumber and mail ship, commanded by Captain G. "Midnight" Olsen.

(*Bottom*) Captain "Midnight" Olsen diving during salvage operations of the *Homer*.

Captain Oscar Oberg mends a sail during the long calm
on voyage from Everett to San Diego, 1905.

Steam schooner *Svea*.

that were blissfully ignored by indifferent operators. At the same time, masters of the steam schooners in many instances were reluctant to cater to passengers. They maintained the ships were operated for the purpose of hauling lumber and lumber products, and not for landlubbers. The situation was not materially aided when passengers boarded ships commanded by such prejudiced skippers, especially when the passengers had been disillusioned by misrepresentations of the ticket agent.[1]

The McCormick Steamship Company went all out in its desire to present comfortable accommodations to persons sailing on their wooden ships. The *Celilo* sported a social hall, tiny as it was, with an electric piano. Many were the nights that passengers stood around this early-day music box and sang as the ship made her way along the coast. Meals were another attraction of this line. They were unsurpassed in quality, and the quantity served was beyond the utmost capacity of most landlubbers. Even waterfront veterans, so often critical of food on ships, had to admit that the McCormick ships were "good feeders."

The coastwise passenger business, of course, did not originate with the steam schooners—nor, in fact, did they originate service to the Mendocino ports. In the middle of the nineteenth century the famous old side-wheelers *Senator, Orizaba,* and *Ancon* were hauling passengers between San Francisco and other Pacific Coast ports. Later came Pacific Coast Steamship Company's dainty little iron *State of California*—to say nothing of their *Queen, Santa Rosa, Curacao,* and *City of Topeka*—and the larger steel steamships *Governor* and *President,* all long popular in the coastwise trade. The Pacific Coast outfit—later "The Admiral Line"—in the 1870's was offering service that included Point Arena, Cuffey's Cove, and Little River. Other companies such as the Oregon Steamship Company, the Occidental Steamship Company, the Pacific Mail Steamship Company, and the Opposition Line provided almost daily sailings to Pacific Northwest and southern

[1] Not all passengers were fussy. Agents tell the story of a two-person stateroom sold to an Oriental who had purchased nine tickets. It would be interesting to know if they took turns sleeping or piled into the bunks—four in one and five in the other.

California ports from San Francisco. New iron steamers such as the *George W. Elder,* the *City of Chester,* the *Ajax,* and the *Oregon* sailed every five days under the Oregon Steamship Line flag for the Northwest, advertising exclusive rights of selling through tickets to emigrants to Oregon at one-half the normal rate, and making connections at Portland with railroads and stages for Idaho Territory. The Opposition Line offered first-class cabin space to Portland for eight dollars and steerage for three dollars; freight was solicited for a dollar a ton. The already ancient *Beaver* had been in operation until 1888, when the old side-wheeler was wrecked.

Several large companies entered the coastwise field when the iron ships went out, replacing them with ships of steel. The San Francisco & Portland Steamship Company, McCormick-owned, operated the steamers *Rose City, Bear,* and *Beaver* from Pier 40, San Francisco. The Pacific Coast Steamship Company offered northbound sailings to Seattle every Wednesday and Saturday on the large offshore liners, *Ruth Alexander, Emma Alexander,* and *H. F. Alexander;* southbound trips to Los Angeles every Monday and Friday. The tariffs were $15.00 and up to Seattle, $7.35 to Los Angeles, and $9.00 to San Diego. Their Portland trade was handled by such steamers as the *Admiral Benson,* the *Admiral Peoples,* and the *Admiral Farragut.*

The story of the *Emma Alexander* is an interesting one. In 1916, while in command of Captain N. Cousins, and with a capacity load of passengers, the ship, then named the *Congress,* caught on fire in the vicinity of Coos Bay. Passengers were removed to ships near by and they safely and more or less comfortably witnessed the destruction of this fine ship. The hull was salvaged and rebuilt as the *Nanking,* entering the trans-Pacific run to the Orient. Shadows of opium smuggling and slave girls crept into the life of this ship—but then, such stories are heard about many vessels that trade to the Far East. At any rate, when the company which ran her went out of business, the *Nanking* was placed on the block, and her old owners bought her back. The *Nanking,* ex-*Congress,* now renamed the *Emma Alexander,* re-entered the coastwise trade. Finally the three fine ships of this company were forced out of business by difficulties of the times.

Near the end of 1910, the Pacific Navigation Company put the former New York–Boston liners *Yale* and *Harvard* on the run between San Francisco, Los Angeles Harbor, and San Diego. That was, of course, before the days of the Panama Canal, and the two white steamers—which resembled excursion vessels more than long-range liners—came out to the coast via the Straits of Magellan. These 21-knot steamers, with good accommodations and a running-time of 25 hours from San Diego to San Francisco, were popular for many years, and their tariff was as low as $8.00 one way, $14.00 for the round trip.

The waterfront strikes of 1934 and 1936, coupled with land transportation competition, led to the withdrawal of the large coastwise liners. The *Harvard* had previously been lost by stranding off Point Arguello, and the *Yale* went to Alaska to serve as a barracks ship for a contractor. The Charles Nelson Company, the Pacific Coast Steamship Company, and the Pacific Navigation Company all folded up, leaving water transportation solely to the few old lumber ships that plied the coast.

11

THE SCANDINAVIAN NAVY

THE coastwise fleet has long been referred to as California's Scandinavian Navy. On any Pacific vessel one can come across a Johnson, a Petersen, or a Liljeborg. The steamer *Alcatraz* operated coastwise for years under skippers by the name of Johnson, Carlson, Fredericksen, Elleson, and Johansen, also the *Brunswick* with captains Andresen, Olsen, Ellefson, and Walgren. All hailed from the Scandinavian countries and all but a few retained their picturesque accent of the land of the Vikings. Swedes, Norwegians, Finns, Danes—all were numerous in the steam-schooner fleet.

Legends, factual and fanciful, have been passed down to substantiate the seamanship of these old-time skippers. Take old Captain "Rain-water Oscar" Johnson, who allegedly navigated his ship on an even keel for two blocks inland on rainwater alone before he realized his mistake, then calmly rang full speed astern and backed out into the stream again. And there was Captain Rohberg, who brought his ship into San Francisco harbor keelside up. This could go on, far into the night.

There were old-time skippers of the steam-schooner fleet who answered to such nicknames as Scantling Bill Roberts, Salvation John Wehman, Hoodlum Bob Walvig, and Flatfoot Hanson. And there was Swell Head Jahnsen, so-called by those who were jealous of him but who was beyond all doubt a superlative skipper and one who taught and guided many a master mariner of later years. And there were, of course, Race Horse John and Caspar Charlie, Berkeley Jim, and Hog Aleck.

Captain Charles Reiner, veteran skipper of the old McCormick fleet and holder of the Congressional Life Saving Medal, can spin many a yarn of life at sea. Outstanding is the time his ship, the *Willamette,* was held up on the high seas by would-be pirates. Reiner refused to elaborate, but old-time waterfront habitués proffered the details.

The *Willamette* had left San Pedro on the evening of December 30, 1913, bound for San Francisco and Northwest ports. On board were twenty-five passengers returning home after the Christmas holidays. Captain Reiner had retired to his cabin and was reviewing the ship's papers when someone knocked on the door, and the skipper bade him to come in. A throaty voice gave the command "Hands up!" and Reiner whirled around, to face an individual wearing a grotesque wig and a false moustache and having a gun in his hand.

Without a thought for himself Reiner made a jump for the gun, and the battle was on. Fortunately it was an automatic, and the slide had been pushed back in such a manner as to make it impossible to fire. The thug pressed the gun into Reiner's ribs and pulled the trigger in vain several times. Captain Reiner was small in stature, and the bandit was slowly overpowering him when the mate and a seaman heard the commotion and, breaking in, subdued the intruder.

An armed confederate was found outside the cabin, and the two were locked in a stateroom until the vessel reached San Francisco, where they were turned over to federal authorities. Investigation disclosed that the pirate leader was in fact a former master mariner who had at one time owned a large schooner and had traded in the Arctic. Some $2,000 was in the safe, and this was thought to have been the goal of the robbers. A map found in their belongings revealed their intention of robbing passengers as well as the ship, beaching the vessel, and escaping in a small launch that had been observed running alongside the *Willamette* during the attempted holdup. The pirates had shadowed Reiner from the time he had left the bank in San Pedro, and had boarded the ship as passengers.

Some fifteen years prior to this incident, Captain Reiner had distinguished himself as a hero, earning the Congressional Life Saving Medal. Reiner was second officer of the coastwise ship *Weott* when that ship struck the Humboldt bar in the year 1899. Reiner took a line ashore through a boiling surf after all other efforts had failed.

Caspar Charlie Carlson, if one is to believe the waterfront legend, once got ashore (this was in his A.B. days) at Astoria, and had himself a liberty which it took all of Astoria's four-man police department to iron out. Only it was the police, rather than Charlie, who received most of the flattening. The next morning, rumor hath it, the judge fined him four dollars and offered him a job on the police force.

Hog Aleck was master of a steam schooner which, on one voyage, found herself with a deckload of hogs on the hoof, all secured in a little pen. She ran into a gale and, as she was old and a bit infirm, she began to go to pieces. Water rose in the hull, her fires went out, and she wallowed, a helpless plaything of the gale. And then she sank. Coast Guardsmen came out in a surfboat to rescue the crew, and among them they found the doughty master, clinging to a bit of shattered wreckage.

When they started to pick him up, they were taken somewhat aback to hear him shout:

"De hell mit me! You safe dem hogs!"

Despite this courteous withdrawal in favor of his grunting ex-cargo, they pulled him into the boat. The story leaked out, as stories always do, and from then on he was Hog Aleck.

Salvation John Wehman was not a particularly pious man. But he reverenced the Salvation Army. Many of his nights in port he spent on a waterfront corner listening to the ear-piercing raucousness of a three-piece "Army" band, staying for the sermon between songs. Captain Wehman, a Russian-Finn, drank heavily of the pastoral lessons, and when the tambourine was passed his gold coin joined the coppers offered by other repentants gathered near.

And then there was Captain Gudmund "Midnight" Olsen, one of the most colorful of skippers and one of the highest-paid masters on the Pacific Coast. For many years Captain Olsen ran the steam schooner *Acme* between San Francisco and Humboldt Bay, carrying lumber, general cargo, and passengers. The *Acme* also served as a mail ship and for that reason Captain Midnight attempted to maintain a regular schedule. Many were the nights when the Humboldt bar was so rough and it was so black that as many as half a dozen ships were either bar-bound or riding outside awaiting daylight and more favorable weather. But not Captain Midnight. He brought the *Acme* into or out of Humboldt Bay often at midnight—thus earning his nickname— through many a curtain of fog or when the bar was so rough that less than six inches remained between keel and solid sand. The little *Acme* was given the name "Flying Dutchman," and her career was colorful. Many were the nights that Midnight brought the *Acme* into port without the inhabitants knowing it until morning, when their mail was awaiting them.

There was a lot of rivalry among bar-bound ships, and when clear weather prevailed many wagers were laid to see which ships would leave Humboldt Bay and be the first to arrive at the Golden Gate. One time after three rough days the steam schooners *San*

Pedro, Acme, Aberdeen, Lakme, and *Point Arena* stood out of Humboldt Bay, Captain Midnight Olsen first with the *Acme* but followed in quick succession by the others. The race was on for San Francisco, with all thought of fuel conservation cast to the winds. The *San Pedro* won the race to San Francisco, with the *Acme* some ten minutes behind, which is close, considering that the race was one of two hundred miles.

But it wasn't always smooth sailing for the *Acme*. Once the bar was so rough—and it must have been rough to stop Captain Midnight—that the little lumber ship was tossed about like a chip on water and the heavy seas grabbed off some 3,000 board feet of the deckload before the ship could make the sheltered waters of the bay. And there was the time when the *Acme* fouled her rudder on some rocks at an open port landing. Captain Midnight, peeling off his clothes and going over the side, dove four times to inspect the rudder himself before he was satisfied to take his ship to sea.

Captain Midnight wasn't deliberately reckless; he knew what he was doing and he knew his ship. Take the time he lay moored off the chute at Greenwood. Old-timers warned Captain Olsen to clear the port, for waves were breaking over Gunderson Rock,[1] and such action meant the harbor was no longer safe for a ship to anchor in. But Captain Midnight was at Greenwood for cargo. He knew that if he stood away from the mooring some other ship might stand in and he would be out his chance to secure a complete load. So Captain Olsen ignored the suggestion of the local people and ordered more lumber on board. Finally, in desperation, the Greenwood lumber people stopped sending lumber, thinking that would move the *Acme* away and outside where she could ride the storm away from dangerous rocks. But the *Acme* remained at Greenwood anchorage and was ready to complete her loading the next morning despite heavy ground swells. Those of Greenwood tell the story and say that it was but the grace of God that saved the *Acme;* but those on board knew that

[1] Named for Captain Thomas "Safe-is-open" Gunderson, commodore of the old L. E. White fleet.

it was with some help of Captain Midnight. Throughout the night the veteran skipper laid on the fo'c'sle head "'feeling" the lines and telling by the surge whether or not it was safe to lay-to at the spot. This was but another occasion when Captain Midnight brought his ship through, loaded lumber, and got under way, considering it but a routine operation.

The *Acme* held records galore. She had the record of making the most trips to Eureka, some forty-eight during the year, with two trips to Coos Bay besides. Then she loaded some 400,000 board feet of lumber in twelve hours, a record for the time. Midnight was unafraid of fog, rain, or heavy weather, and all ports were the same to him. He brought his ship into San Francisco during a heavy fog at 1:00 A.M. and by 10:30 that same evening he had unloaded his cargo of lumber, had taken on a cargo of merchandise and passengers and was on his way to Eureka.

In later years Captain Olsen was the master of the salvage ship *Homer* and made a name for himself with several spectacular salvage jobs. The *Homer,* a converted steam schooner, pulled the tank ship *Frank H. Buck* off Monterey rocks; she later pulled the United States destroyer *DeLong* off the sands at Half Moon Bay; and she helped her sister ship, the *Iaqua,* in salvage work on the Dutch ship *Malakka.* The large motor ship was on her maiden voyage when she struck Cedros Island off Mexico. This fine new ship was the latest in marine appointments; even the crew quarters were finished in solid mahogany, and the tableware bore the crest of the Crown Prince. Tons of canned goods, beans, and coffee were taken from this salvage job.

Captain Midnight Olsen retired from the sea, purchased an interest in a famous Lake County resort, and spends his time supposedly looking after his establishment; but more than likely is kept busy with second-generation sea-minded youngsters priming him for yarns of the days when he was sailing the redwood coast.

Captain "Hurry-up" Jack Bostrom, late master of such steam schooners as the *National City, Coquille River,* and *Arctic,* was an impatient skipper earning his nickname by forever being in a hurry to get loaded and under way. In later years "Hurry-up" Jack earned another name, that of "Saturday-night" Jack. It seems that Captain Bostrom waited until he was well along in years before he learned to dance. Once master of the light fantastic, Captain Bostrom presented the early-day version of "cutting a mean rug." He always tried to arrange his ship's schedule so as to make Fort Bragg on Saturday night for the large country dances held there. If in port he often lay over under some pretense of maintenance work or other excuse. And it was said that no dance was complete without Captain Bostrom, for "Saturday-night" Jack really had a good time.

"Hoodlum Bob" Walvig, master of the early-day steam schooners *Newsboy, Cleone, Point Arena,* and *Scotia,* was no hoodlum. Rather he earned his name being handy with his fists. In the early days of coastwise sailing there were sailors who, on frequent occasions, took exception to orders. It was then that Captain Walvig took over, working the "Hoodlum" over, as he called them, until he was willing to carry out orders.

J. S. Higgins, master of the *Silver Spring* and *South Coast* as well as later steam schooners, was of all things an ordained minister, so they say. Now a man of the cloth chose a strange career when he entered seafaring life, and very often would undoubtedly cringe amid the blue air of salty manifestations of profanity. Captain Higgins' position was no different. Many were the mornings that he could be found on deck praying for the salvation of his ornery crew, who perhaps had tangled with Finn loggers in one of the ports of call the previous night.

"Port-wine" John Ellefsen, master of the *Brunswick,* was a genteel person who leaned more toward the cultural side of life than to the abrupt way of the regular seafaring men. In those days it was common for skippers of the coast to carry a gallon jug of whiskey for use as an occasional bracer after hard days of loading. One of the practices of the steam-schooner fleet was that of having loading and unloading done by the crew rather than by longshoremen. Many ports did not have manpower

96

sufficient to handle loading operations. So the crew carried out this work. And often after a long day of sailing in heavy weather they would turn to and take on a load of lumber without rest. So you can see that, while they possibly stretched the reason for taking a bracer now and then, the steam-schooner boys did work hard. Whiskey was used for smoothing over arguments with shoreside talesmen who checked the lumber, and for medicinal purposes, both internally and externally. Captain Ellefsen frowned on this practice of serving hard liquor, and he may have been right. The custom in those days was to serve whiskey, not in a so-called shot glass, but in a jelly glass. And any skipper who served less than half a jelly glass at a time was considered cheap. "Port-wine" John was not cheap but, seldom drinking himself, could not stand to pass out fire-water in that quantity. Yet he wanted to be sociable and be one of the boys. So what did he do but carry along a supply of port wine. And, strong liquor or not, "Port-wine" John did have a host of friends along the redwood coast.

Captain Thomas "Safe-is-open" Gunderson was one of the real old-time skippers. He commanded such early-day steam schooners as the *Alcazar* and in later years the *Helen P. Drew*. Operating between Greenwood and San Francisco for the L. E. White Lumber Company, Captain Gunderson learned every crag and submerged rock between the two ports. There is a rock at Greenwood named after Captain Gunderson, and when waves break over this rock Greenwoodites say it is time to move your ship away from the jagged rocks and out to the open sea, for it is certain a storm is brewing. Captain Gunderson earned his name by calling the bluff of many a young upstart in his crew who threatened to quit when the going got tough for them. "So you want to quit, huh? Well, that suits me. Come up to my room. The safe is always open. I'll pay you off!" Few of them ever took the opportunity to quit; rather, they stopped their griping and resumed their work.

Captain "Whispering" Winkle had an operation on his throat which left him with little more than a whisper of a voice, hence his nickname. Captains "Big Sharkey" Hendricksen and "Little Sharkey" Gallis were so called from their resemblance to the old-time fighter Tom Sharkey, in both profile and fisticability.

There was "Red Charlie" Thorsell, a short, heavy man with a fiery crop of red hair. And there was "Flatfoot" Hanson, who sported a long black beard. And then there were "Nosey" Higgins, "Danish Prince" Hansen, and "Pie-face" Johnson, many of them veterans of the Mendocino City–Fort Bragg–San Francisco run for the Union Lumber Company fleet.

And now comes the time when many of the steam-schooner complement must hang their heads in shame. A few—and it may be safely stated quite a few—of the crew members saw how to make considerable money on the side in the shady business of transporting hard liquors from foreign ports, such as those in Mexico and Canada, to the then dry United States, made dry by the unpopular Eighteenth Amendment. Now it was perfectly legal—or at least tolerable—for the skippers to have their usual gallon supply of whiskey on board—there was always the chance that some husky crew member might get a bit upset, say a stomach ache, and there is nothing like whiskey to cure a seaman's ailment, internally or externally. However, the law put its foot down on shipload lots of whiskey. No crew was ever that sick. So there were numerous brushes with the law.

On one occasion the entire engine-room crew of the steam schooner *Helene* was arrested by Hoquiam, Washington, police for having nine cases of liquor on board. Then there was the *Chehalis,* also raided at Hoquiam and charged with having a case of booze on board. Then it was the *G. C. Lindauer* which ran into difficulty when the law found, among some fifty sacks of coal, some six sacks of Old Hermitage brand.

The *Multnomah* had a run-in with Portland police and her personnel was charged with bootlegging when a cache was found in the engine room. And the Grays Harbor, Washington, supply of Christmas spirits suffered a setback when the *Svea* and *Grays Harbor* were visited by the law; some twenty cases of whiskey were taken from the *Grays Harbor,* and over one hundred quarts were seized on the *Svea*. The liquor on the *Grays Harbor* was found in a double bulkhead in the captain's and mate's quarters. It seems that the *Grays Harbor* had several brushes with the law, for she had been raided only a month previously and had then lost forty-five quarts of whiskey. Not all the raids were successful—successful that is, for the police. The *Carlos,* the *Daisy Gadsby,* and the *Hoquiam* were all boarded but either trod the straight and narrow or else knew their bulkhead caches. One engineer on board the *Brooklyn* evidently had a wholesale business with agents in each port; for when he was caught, through the medium of one of his shoreside agents, he was fined $500 and given a five-month jail sentence. It was said along the San Francisco waterfront that when certain steam schooners were in port all the facilities of a "blind pig" were proffered the waterfront habitués who held a thirst. And one steward on board the *Daisy Gadsby* allegedly enjoyed an income several times that of the master—that is, until he was caught by company personnel and fired.

They were a hardy, competent, hell-roaring crew, who took their whiskey straight (perhaps with a beer chaser) but who knew how to handle it, and there are no records indicating that dalliance with the derivatives of rye or corn had any bearing on their actions at sea. Deepwater officers may be inclined to look down their noses at their brethren of the coastal routes, and it is probably true that in the "Scandinavian Navy" there were many whose celestial navigation knew no such refinements as Weems, Ageton Dreisonstock—or even Marc Saint Hilaire. But for the ordinary rough-and-tumble of putting a ship into an anchorage which would make your deepwater sailor wake up screaming, they were without equal. And their navigation was ample for their needs.

It may have been a bit informal; there is one tale of a steam-schooner master who was endeavoring to teach a bit of navigation to a sailor, and made this epic statement:

"I takes me a lonnitude, und from dat I works out a ladditude. If it don't come out vere I t'ink ve should be—vy, de hell mit dat lonnitude und I takes me anudder vun!"

12

THEN CAME SHIPS OF STEEL

SHORTLY after the turn of the century there came a sharp increase in the demand for pine lumber and the forests of Oregon and Washington began to attract many new mill operators. Men who had pioneered in redwood operation on the northern California coast expanded their operations into the pine forests along the Columbia River, at Grays Harbor, at Coos Bay, and on Puget Sound. Foremost among these operators from the Mendocino coast and Humboldt Bay were Charles McCormick, Andrew Hammond, Robert Dollar, and Charles Nelson.

It was this northerly migration which spelled the end of the little steam schooners as far as their domination of the coastal lumber field was concerned. Built for the relatively short voyages between the Mendocino dog-holes and the more southerly ports of California, they were neither strong enough nor long-legged enough for runs which took in the entire western seaboard of the United States.[1] It became simply a matter of having ships with more cargo space, greater strength, and larger bunkers. Men operated the wooden ships as long as they dared, until steam schooners with their engines amidships began to shoulder the "stem-winders" aside; but there is a limit to all things, and, generally speaking, the limit for seagoing wooden ships is a length of about two hundred feet. Everyone thought that McCormick was going too far when he built the twin-screw *Everett*—she was 236 feet long—and the launching of Hart-Wood's 241-foot *San Diego* raised eyebrows all along California Street. What it all sums up to is this: a wooden hull has a great deal of resiliency —so much so, in fact, that if she is too long her ends are going to sag, giving her a mildly humpbacked silhouette which is both distasteful to the eye and conducive to spewed oakum and resultant leakage. The only way to prevent it is by filling the hold so full of heavy timbers that little room will remain for cargo.

Although better known as the founder of a line of globe-circling steamships, the late Captain Robert Dollar also was a lumberman of Usal, California. And he was one of the earliest advocates of the steel steam schooner, which was the obvious answer to the need for bigger, more profitable ships. The doughty captain, who was nothing if not an astute businessman, contracted for the construction, in the Puget Sound yards of the Moran Company, of three steel steam schooners of 1,800 gross tons, 240 feet in length, each having a capacity of better than 1,500,000 board feet of lumber. He kept one of them—the *Stanley Dollar*—and sold the other two, the *Falcon* and the *Riverside,* to Charles Nelson Company. He tried to interest Fred Linderman in the deal, but Linderman wasn't any too anxious to go experimenting in steel until he had seen how it was going to work. Other operators, however, soon began to augment their fleets with steel ships.

---

[1] The ventures of steam schooners into the Alaska trade at the time of the gold rush of 1898 were successful only because a gold-seeker will travel in anything, regardless of safety and comfort. Besides, in those days, steamboat inspectors were more easygoing.

Olson & Mahoney built the steel steam schooner *Olson & Mahoney*, the E. J. Dodge Company ordered the steel *St. Helens*, and finally Linderman came out with the steel *Cricket*. This last, built by the United Engineering Company of Alameda, had several features which were new to the field but later were adopted by other operators. The Linderman and the Nelson vessels were both under supervision of the same port engineer. Linderman watched the operations of the *Riverside* and the *Falcon*, noticing they both loaded by the head, with unequal work placed on loading gears, the forward gear receiving the bulk of the work. The *Cricket* came out with boilers on the main deck abaft the engines. San Francisco's waterfront was greatly excited over this innovation; they said it would be top-heavy. Nevertheless the new design allowed some 200,000 more board feet to be carried in the longer deck space and the longer hold.

The new steel ships were faster, for by now the triple-expansion engine had replaced the simple compounds. Moreover, each had two boilers at least and the chief engineer no longer had to wire down the safety-valve if he wanted more steam. Another thing in favor of the new ones was the great reduction of the fire hazard—which, of course, caused them to be regarded with a far less jaundiced eye by the insurance people; and when the underwriters are favorably impressed, you pay less for your insurance. This cut the operating costs considerably. On top of that, the steam schooners now could transport deadweight cargoes of sugar, salt, cement, and other commodities which simply cannot be handled in a ship where there is any chance of leaky seams. Also eliminated were the menaces of marine borers, rot, certain seagoing cousins of the termites, and other things which are likely to afflict a wooden ship from the time she is launched until she becomes old and nailsick. On top of all this, the steel ship has far less of her internal space taken up by thick frames and ceiling, knees, keelsons, and other massive bits of woodwork. That means much more room for cargo—and more room for cargo means more profit.

Passenger accommodations in the steel ships were better than

Pasadena, first steam schooner on Pacific Coast
to use oil as fuel.

Willamette, combination passenger-cargo steam schooner
on her maiden voyage.

Loading offshore cargo ship by wire-chute method, Noyo Harbor, 1926.

those in the wooden ones—they had to be, in order to meet competition of the offshore iron steamers operating between San Francisco and Puget Sound. The *Camino* carried 87 passengers; the *Olson & Mahoney* packed 75, and so it went, down the line to the two which were accommodated aboard the *Cricket,* in a degree of relative luxury which approached what one would expect in an owner's suite. Linderman, incidentally, stuck strictly to the freight business, leaving the lucrative but often headachey transportation of human beings to other operators.[2]

By now, steel was on the upswing, although wooden construction continued for a decade. The year 1911 saw a dozen steel-hulled ships among the total of 126 lumber carriers along the coast, and in 1913 there were 26 steel ones among the then total of 155 vessels. Riveters and plate rollers and chippers continued their slow but steady advance on the ranks of the carpenters and caulkers, as the new idea caught on. However, ship operation is affected by tradition, and the transition was not a rapid one.

In 1923, the *Esther Johnson* was built—a 1,041-ton vessel with her machinery amidships, and with a carrying capacity of 1,275,000 board feet. When she slid down the Matthews' way at Portland, Oregon, on that October day more than a score of years ago, she marked the end of an era; the *Esther Johnson* was the last of the wooden steam schooners. That was the definite break in the period which saw a proportion of three wooden ships to every steel one in operation—but as late as 1925 there still were a hundred wooden steamers in service.

The cessation of hostilities at the close of World War I gave added impetus to the use of steel, for hundreds upon hundreds of brand-new steel ships were lying idle in the backbay waters of American ports. The United States Shipping Board had completed a program of building the greatest wartime maritime fleet the world had ever known—but with the war at an end there was little new tonnage to attract operators, and ships that had

[2] These headaches included the large number of Important Persons who insisted on a place at the captain's table, the ones with children who got in everyone's hair, and the drunks who fell down the hatches and then sued the owners.

never felt the slap of sea water, or even of fresh water, were destined to rust away. The government, in an effort to stimulate interest in the use of these ships, placed them on the market at what were definitely bargain-counter rates. Ships costing well over two million dollars often went for less than a hundred thousand, and subsidies in the form of mail contracts were proffered in sales where ships were to be used in foreign trade. Almost every coastwise operator took advantage of this chance with new ships to replace his obsolete and aged wooden ones. McCormick disposed of his last two wooden ships, the *Celilo* and the *Wapama,* and purchased some thirty steel ships for coastwise, intercoastal, and world-wide operation. The majority of steel Shipping Board vessels that were acquired by coastwise operators were of the small "Point" and "Lake" types, both so-called from the prefixes to their names. They were 250 feet in length and carried around a million and a half board feet of lumber. The conventional two masts were removed, and in their places were installed four masts for loading. One mast was placed on the forecastle head and another on the poop, while the remaining two were installed amidships, one forward and one abaft the superstructure. In a few, two sets of king posts were installed in lieu of the main and mizzenmasts.

Despite the fact that the steel ships operated in larger bodies of water and were not subjected to the hazards of Mendocino dog-hole navigation, they did occasionally meet with accidents, and there were disasters that were as sensational as those which had befallen the pioneer wooden vessels. More than one steel ship met her doom when she steamed too close in and her bottom was ripped wide open on the rocks that line the coastal steamer lanes.

And then there was the *Falcon*. For years she operated coastwise in the service of the Nelson flag; then she went to work for Andrew F. Mahoney, former partner in the Olson & Mahoney firm. Laid up because of lack of business, the *Falcon,* by this time renamed the *Santa Inez,* entered the fishing trade as a mother ship to a group of whale boats. The poor old *Santa Inez* reeked with the pungent odor of cooked whale oil, processed in retorts on the deck of the ship, and other ships gave her as wide a berth as early-day clipper ships had given the stinking "black bird" slave traders of the Gold Coast.

Then came lean years. The *Santa Inez* was laid up and was eventually sold to Thailand. Waterfront gossip has it that the *Santa Inez* has been lost during this war off the China Coast.

The *Santa Elisa* was loading scrap iron, destined for Japan, in San Francisco when the war in the Orient broke out in 1937. The Chinese crew on board the *Santa Elisa* promptly walked off the ship; they returned later, although they refused to sail her with cargo destined to be used against their native land. Investigation revealed that the ship was owned by Japanese interests, and American groups, fired by respect and loyalty for China, promptly threw a picket line around her—you know what a picket line means to a longshoreman. Finally they moved the *Santa Elisa* out into the stream and took off the Japanese in her complement, but left the Chinese aboard. The days dragged into weeks, the weeks into months, and finally the months into years. The Chinese Consul kept them fed, meanwhile wrangling with the Japanese interests through intermediaries. Then the ship was sold to Sir Walter Carpenter of Australia, and she is said to be still operating in the South Seas.

One of the outstanding steel steam schooners was the *Scotia*, ex-*Lake Galewood*, which was operated for a number of years by the Pacific Lumber Company, and ran between Field's Landing, on Humboldt Bay, and ports as far south as San Diego. Her owners were far ahead of the times in the matter of providing crew quarters, which approached the luxurious, and in seeing to it that she was "a good feeder." Under the genial command of the late Captain Alex McKenzie, the *Scotia* was a home as well as a job; in fact, so highly was she regarded that in one case, the master of another steam schooner forsook his berth in order to go third mate in the *Scotia*. But good food, good pay, and good quarters smack of "dangerous paternalism"; it was noted that members of her crew who had been aboard for many months would suddenly ask to be signed off because of an ailing wife or a moribund grandmother. Finally her owners chartered her to an overseas concern, and she eventually wound up in government service.

Among the last of the steam schooners to operate along the coast were the famous *Noyo* (No.2) and the *Noyo* (No. 3). The former, a beautiful little steel single-ender, had originally been the passenger-cargo steamer *Aroline* and was later the *Admiral Goodrich*. She was fast—good for thirteen knots—and her staterooms were above average. When she went to pieces in the fog off Point Arena in 1932, not so very far from where the original, wooden *Noyo* came to her end, she was replaced by the third *Noyo*. The last one, purchased from Nelson, originally was the *Griffdu*. But her career, too, was short. Her operators, the National Steamship Company, found the going a bit tough in the Fort Bragg–southern California trade and sold her to Thailand.

Today, only a handful of lumber carriers remains, with steel ships hardly more plentiful than wood in the coastwise trade. Many of them have been diverted to special wartime uses and to operations far from the dog-holes of Mendocino. With them have gone their hardy and practical skippers—diamonds in the rough—just as they went in World War I. In that conflict, incidentally, the government took over many of the larger steam schooners, commissioning the officers in the Naval Reserve and, so the legend goes, adding the prefix "U.S.S." to the vessels' names. This latter proved, in some cases, a bit puzzling—but the men of the Scandinavian Navy carried it off with a flourish. Witness the murky night when one of the "Lake" steam schooners, leaving the mouth of the Thames, inadvertently passed on the wrong side of a British picket boat:

"What ship is that?" hailed a British rating, by megaphone. There was only silence from the American vessel. The hail was repeated—a bit sharply—but brought no more response than before. *Wham!* A one-pounder shot cut across the bow of the passing vessel. Immediately there came a jangle of bells from the steamer's engine room, followed by the thrashing of her propeller in reverse. From her darkened bridge, an angry Scandinavian voice came across the water:

"Dees iss United Staats var-sheep *Lake Erie*—und ve vill haff no more of dat!"

Clangety-clang! Clangety-clang! Again the freighter's master rang "Ahead-full," and with dignified silence, the *Lake Erie* passed on into the night.

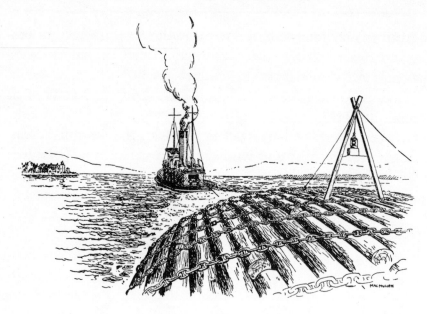

13

COME TO ME, GO FROM ME

TUGBOAT companies are not in business from motives of altruism. It costs money, plenty of it, to keep a fleet of tugs in service, with steam up and crews ready, just to be on hand when they are needed. This is a fact which owners and masters of sailing vessels seldom took into account as they rent the air with their anguished wails at the expense involved in, let us say, getting a loaded barkentine from somewhere off the Farallones to a snug berth at Crockett or Benicia or South San Francisco—or perhaps an empty hull from Mendocino County to Oakland.

As a result, a bit of towing was done now and then by the steam schooners. Of course, they couldn't chisel in on the really big jobs, for the ordinary steam schooner didn't have any too much power to get herself up and down the coast in the teeth of a decent breeze, let alone to accomplish it with something hanging from a hawser out over her fantail.

Steam-schooner towing goes back a long way. In fact, it was away back in 1888 that the *South Coast* took on a ferryboat-delivery job from San Francisco to San Diego. Her tow was a little flat-bottomed ferry called the *Benicia,* which had been a cattle boat running around the Benicia-Martinez area. The *South Coast* hauled her from San Francisco as far south as San Pedro, where, the weather being fine and the seas moderate, they lighted off the *Benicia's* little locomotive-type boiler and she went on to San Diego on her own, her diminutive walking-beam nodding gravely to passing seagulls during the eighty-mile run in the open sea.

Few of the steam schooners had towing engines[1] and had therefore to depend upon various home-made devices to keep an even strain and thus avoid either snapping the towline or ripping out the towing-bitts while the tow was climbing up a sea and the towing vessel was sliding downhill on the other side. One favorite trick was to make the towline fast, not to the bitts on the vessel being towed, but rather to fifteen or twenty fathoms of anchor-chain. The chain, being heavy, of course had a tendency to hang down, deep in the water, and increased strain would raise it toward the surface, giving a sort of spring effect and cushioning the load. It worked very nicely.

The *Wapama* was one steam schooner which carried a towing engine, and she added a bit to her owners' revenue by now and then doubling as a towboat at attractive rates. Perhaps her most picturesque effort along these lines was in 1926 when she got the job of towing the Alaska Packers Association's old bark *Star of India* down from San Francisco, to become San Diego's maritime museum.

The little steam schooner *National City* fell into a bit of luck —and cash—in 1902, when she stumbled upon the dismasted

[1] The towing engine—known in the vernacular as a "Come to me, go from me" —is a sort of winch, consisting of a steam engine and a large drum on which the towing-wire is wound. As soon as the desired length of wire is run out to the tow, the device is set to take up slack if the strain eases and pay out wire as a sudden load comes up, thereby equalizing the strain on the wire—as well as on the tug and her tow.

German bark *Otto Gildemeister*, wallowing off the southern California coast. The German vessel, whose master apparently belonged to the old school of sail-crackers, must have hung to his canvas a bit too long on a passage from Japan to the Columbia. Anyhow, her sticks went over the side, and she drifted down almost to San Diego, where the *National City* found her and snaked her into port. There was, of course, a bit of salvage involved here, rather than a bargain-counter towing job. The *Otto Gildemeister*, incidentally, lived to sail again, first as the *Homeward* and later as the *Star of Holland*, of Alaska Packers.

The steam schooners *Chehalis* and *Norwood* were making their way down the coast in the face of heavy weather when they came across the passenger ship *City of Puebla* wallowing in the troughs, with engines disabled and some two hundred passengers on board violently seasick from the heavy rolling. It was a January night of 1906 and the winter winds seemed to howl with particular delight as they rocked the liner full of landlubbers. The freighter *Charles Nelson* was standing by the *City of Puebla*, and had had a line on board her; but owing to breaking a steam pipe the *Charles Nelson* was unable to do much more than hold her own in the gale.

The little *Chehalis* and *Norwood* inched their way toward the liner, and each succeeded in getting a line on board. Soon the lumber schooners were headed south with the Seattle–San Francisco liner in tow. Everything went well until the group came to the entrance of San Francisco's Golden Gate, when the master of the *City of Puebla* suddenly cast off the lines of the steam schooners and called for a commercial tug. Now one may imagine the surprise and dismay of the lumber skippers at such a move. Without doubt they had optimistic ideas concerning salvage money when they reached port with this good-sized ship. They say that passengers who were on board the liner still cringe and clap hands to their ears at the very mention of the discussion that went on between the lumber skippers and the master of the *City of Puebla* off the San Francisco heads when the towlines were cast off.

Greenwood Anchorage.

Greenwood wire-chute landing.

Albion Mill, 1923.

MAC MULLEN PHOTOS

Rotten Row, Oakland Creek.

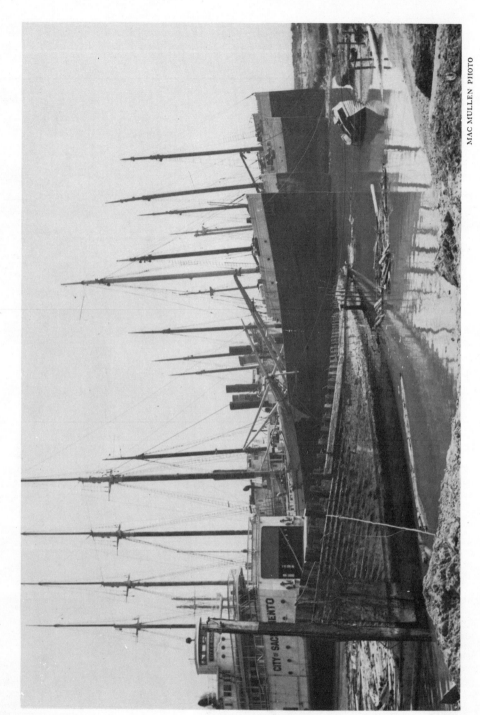

Slowly they fall apart.

Other incidents involved steam schooners and the salvage of sailing ships. The steam schooner *Northland* salvaged the British bark *Melanope* off the Oregon coast in 1906 and towed her to Astoria. And there was the bark *Ferris S. Thompson* in trouble in the Potato Patch and towed to the safety of San Francisco Bay in 1900 by the steam schooner *Homer*. The steam schooner *Riverside* salvaged the schooner *Defender* off the Mendocino coast in 1913 and towed her to San Francisco. Time and again, too, the steam schooners were of assistance to one another. They would either lose a propeller or snap a tailshaft and, often drifting dangerously toward the beach, would be rescued by a sister steam schooner just in the nick of time.

Many of the steam schooners were built at out-of-the-way dog-holes where there were no facilities for installing engines and boilers; it was necessary, under these circumstances, to tow the empty hull to San Francisco, where some iron works, such as Fulton, would take over the job of putting in the machinery. Thus the *Chehalis*, the *Helen P. Drew*, the *Martha Buehner*, the *Merced*, the *Yosemite*, and the *Yellowstone* were towed by sister ships to San Francisco for completion. Often the new hull was loaded with lumber and towed with a pay load to San Francisco. The *Helen P. Drew* made such a maiden voyage to San Francisco from Greenwood fully loaded with ties from the L. E. White mills. In San Francisco, Fulton Iron Works installed a small compound engine in the little lumber ship.

And now comes a phase of coastwise towing which, while not involving the ships of the redwood coast—at least, directly—was a colorful angle of the Western lumber industry for many years. This was the business of the seagoing log rafts, of which the ones towed from the Columbia to San Diego were the largest and the most celebrated.

The steam-schooner people didn't like the log rafts. The maritime unions liked them even less; for one powerful tug could handle the same amount of lumber which would have filled a dozen steam schooners at least. That, of course, meant fewer jobs.

The rafts of logs were made up, in cradles at Cathlanet, on the

Columbia, the work being done during the winter months when not even the most starry-eyed optimist would think of undertaking a long offshore tow job with such a load. When it was all finished, the raft was a cigar-shaped affair from 900 to 1,000 feet long—a big bundle of logs including around 5,000,000 board feet of lumber. The whole thing was held together with a veritable network of chains, big chains at that; discarded anchor-chain was the favorite type. Down through the middle ran another long chain to the bow-end of which the towing-wire was made fast with a shackle. At the stern end the chain, also fitted with a shackle, was carried up to the top of the raft and held in place with stoppers; the idea was, of course, that if anything went wrong at the forward end and the chain parted, the tug could go around to the stern and find something else to which it might secure.

By way of superstructure the rafts generally carried a deck-load of telephone poles. Near each end there was an X-shaped frame from which hung a white lantern, lighted either from a storage-battery in a box fastened to the bottom of the lantern or from a small flask of acetylene gas. This not only gave warning to passing traffic but also enabled those on the tug to keep track of their tow at night.

Along in the early summer the first of the rafts would be towed out of the Columbia and would head down the coast to San Diego, where the Benson Lumber Company's mill was ready to receive them, break them up, and saw the logs into dimension lumber. It was a long and somewhat disagreeable job, lasting from two to three weeks—sixty miles was considered an excellent 24-hour run. There is nothing more depressing than seeing and feeling a powerful reciprocating engine turning up for full speed, but getting no more speed than, as often, two knots. The mate on one of the tugs once summed it up in a few words:

"You turn in at night, und dere iss a lighthouse outside your cabin vindow. In de morning you gets up—and dere, py Yesus, iss de same dam' lighthouse! You stand und talk mit somebody until you get sick of him, so you valk avay. You go around de deckhouse—und you run right into him head-on. Dese tugs iss so little you can't get away from nobotty!"

Back on the East Coast, long-range log-rafting had been tried as far back as 1888, when some zealot made up a huge bundle of logs in Maine and—if you can imagine such a thing—put masts into it, and rigged it as a four-masted bark. It wasn't what you would call a howling success, and we heard no more of that sort of thing.

A log raft was launched at Fort Bragg in May of 1892. It was some 600 feet long, 35 feet wide, and 20 feet deep. Some difficulty was experienced in handling this mass of logs. Maneuvering a floating object 600 feet long in a dog-hole scarcely larger in size is no picnic. But they got her to sea and on her way to San Francisco, only to have her chains give way. A great many logs were lost, but a small portion of the raft was towed to San Francisco, thus paving a way for similar shipments.

The first log raft to go from the Columbia to San Diego was in 1906, towed on a 12-inch hemp hawser.[2] Hemp, of course, is likely to break—and it did—so it wasn't long before they began using wire and towing engines; the wire was about as thick as your wrist. And so it went on, for years, with Red Stack tugs generally performing the work. At times as many as five rafts would be sent south each season, the tug pausing only long enough between trips to take on bunkers and supplies.

There was surprisingly little trouble with the rafts. Once in a great while an unheralded storm would come up, a raft would get loose, and on occasion would even break up. This, of course, was just what the steamship people were waiting for, as it gave them a lovely opportunity to talk about the hazard created by floating logs. But the breakups were negligible; aside from a tug occasionally running out of fuel on a long-drawn-out tow and having to radio for help while she scuttled into San Francisco or San Pedro to refill her tanks, it was an uneventful business— at least up to the end of the service.

[2] Hemp is measured by circumference, a 12-inch hawser being about four inches thick. Wire rope is measured by diameter.

Along in 1940, the trouble began. For no reason which will ever be clear, one of the rafts caught fire, off Monterey, and was badly damaged. And the next year the same thing happened, in just about the same place. Now, if you cannot understand how a raft of wet logs can catch fire with the seas washing over it, don't feel badly; there are several thousand well-informed, intelligent people who can't figure it out either. When you consider the fact that all that lumber going to San Diego was of definite importance to the defense effort, you will appreciate the fact that there were many who would have tried to stop it by fair means or foul, preferably the latter.

At any rate, the raft which caught fire in the early summer of 1941 was the last of the lot.

14

ROTTEN ROW

THERE are many maritime graveyards in obscure waters of the Pacific Coast where lie the ships that are too old and decrepit to be of further use. But the mudflats of Oakland Creek, on San Francisco Bay, stand out as the Arlington of marine graveyards. Laymen regard the tied-up ships with aversion—to them the old vessels are "eyesores" in contrast to surrounding shoreside architecture. But Pacific Coast mariners figuratively tip their caps in reverence as they pass these occupants of the tidal flats.

In this backwater of San Francisco Bay lies the largest group of old, weather-beaten, wooden steam schooners. Their once white superstructures are gray and chalky, bared of paint in many spots by the winds. Rotted rope-falls hang from davits; rotted canvas exposes the once buoyant cork of life rings. Vents are badly pitted. One stack has rusted through.

A ghostly stillness surrounds the old ships. Empty decks and vacant cabins lend eeriness to this marine graveyard. Missing is the noisy clatter of cargo winches, long frozen by rust. These matriarchs of the merchant marine lie silent, with the tides caressing their dock-scarred sides; they must be satisfied to ride the swells of an occasional passing tug.

An unrecognizable hulk of an early-day ship—some say it is the *Mayfair*—lies half buried in the mud ahead of the other vessels. Astern, almost awash, is the wreckage of another veteran, identified—God only knows how—as the *Phoenix*. On the beach are heavy planks and beams, square-cut and with iron fittings that could have come only from a sailing ship later converted to steam; perhaps it was the *Arcata*. These maritime outcasts are examples of the probable fate of the rest of the mudflat fleet, for years of idleness have preyed on planks and engines. It is extremely doubtful if any of these ships will ever up-anchor and stand out to the open sea; it is far more likely that they will remain as decaying manifestations of the days when tiny ships formed an important part of Pacific Coast shipping.

Shrouds hang disconsolately from split, useless masts. Turnbuckles that secured many a deckload of lumber lie rusted on racks under the forecastle heads. A broken boom lies on a forward deck, making one wonder about the strength of the remaining booms. Lifeboat gear is in place but rotted beyond use. Truly, this mudflat fleet is a dismal contrast to the present-day maritime activity. Men of the sea, without derision, refer to this final resting place of forgotten ships as "Rotten Row."

The first Rotten Row came about during the early days of San Francisco. Sailing craft, left to rot in the Bay while gold-hungry skippers and crew members headed for the Diggin's, were finally towed out of the way of Bay traffic. Many of the ships found their way to the beaches near Hunter's Point; these were the decaying hulks that were too far gone to be of service. Others were in good condition and were towed to sheltered waters such as Oakland Creek. The masters, who were often the owners, lived on the ships and kept them in readiness for sea when occasion arose. Many are the tales—tall and colorful—that were told to youngsters of the area by these doughty men of the sea; more than one future marine career resulted from the stories passed along by the old veterans of sail to impressionable lads. But the "occasion" whereby the sailing craft could have been used never came about. Steam had come to stay, and the old ships and barks and schooners were resigned to the dismal fate of rotting away. And so came about "Rotten Row."

Like the sailing craft whose place they had taken, the steam schooners also grew old and obsolete; they, too, met their fate in the mudflats. But "Rotten Row" was not restricted to wooden ships. The years following World War I were slack for shipping and brought large offshore vessels into "Rotten Row." Unlike ships of wood, the steel vessels were of some use even after being condemned to marine scrapheaps. Their hulls were torn apart and sent to the steel mills. Only one ship of steel remains in Oakland Creek today, and this one is being held for speculation and possible service again, rather than for scrapping.

Ships of wood, once stripped of boilers and engines, are of little use. A few have been made into barges. Some have been filled with mud and used as breakwaters in small harbors. The rest lie on the flats with their planks falling apart and the tides washing them away, piece by piece.

The vessels lie moored with bows nosed into the south shore. It is easy at first sight to imagine they are awaiting sailing orders; but such fanciful thoughts are shattered when one surveys the old wagons close aboard.

There is the *Svea,* a steam schooner of some forty years' vintage, fifteen of them in "'Rotten Row." Her superstructure is badly stained by fuel oil and her iron ladders have corroded. Dry rot is in evidence, and she bears all the marks of having been on the bottom. The *Svea,* named after one of the two political divisions of Sweden when that country was divided, once stood into port, keelside up and under tow, after having been in collision with an offshore vessel. But even after that, she was repaired and operated in coastwise service for years. The old-timer's troubles went on even after she reached the comparative safety of the mudflats. A heavy wind blew her against an underwater piling, which stove in several planks, and she sank. She was pumped out and drydocked, and her hull was made sound again; but that was as far as repairs went. Her superstructure is still in a sorry state—even without the still visible "high-tide mark" left by floating oil.

Alongside the *Svea* are her two sister ships, the *Oregon* and the *Idaho*. Like the *Svea* they haven't seen service for many years, but they are in considerably better condition. These three ships are remnants of the once large fleet of sailing and steamships of Wilson Brothers, Grays Harbor lumbermen.

In the spring of 1929 the *Svea* stood into San Francisco Bay, and on orders from the owners was taken over to Oakland Creek for what was to have been a temporary lay-up. She moored alongside several other ships, paid off the crew, but kept a skeleton force of officers. Soon other steam schooners moored alongside, including the *Oregon* and *Idaho*. Steam was even maintained on a few of the ships, for all believed this inactivity to be short-lived.

Gradually came the realization that the country was in the throes of a depression and that there was little chance for the ships to see service for some time. Officers were dismissed, and only the masters were retained.

Shoreside commander of the mudflat fleet is the former master of the *Svea,* Captain Karl Rohberg—a rotund little mariner with a pleasant smile and a nautical way about him. Captain Rohberg has served under the Wilson flag in both sail and steam for thirty-five years, fifteen of them in the mudflats. He sailed with the *Svea* when she was in coastwise service, when she was requisitioned by the government during World War I for the Central American mahogany trade, and again when she returned to the West Coast. He was with her when she capsized off the southern California coast after a collision, and he remained with her even after her lay-up.

The Wilson fleet has been a victim of more than the depression. During the lay-up the owner died, and the heirs, successful in their own professions, doubted the feasiblity of putting the ships back into service. This has kept them at the mudflats—but not abandoned. Captain Rohberg has been retained on full pay for the entire period of the lay-up, to watch over the fleet. The ships are not for sale, and any suggestion that they be scrapped is coldly rejected. So there they lie—and Captain Rohberg probably is the only skipper in command of a vessel which has not sailed in fifteen years.

Queen of the mudflat fleet is the little passenger-cargo steamer *Celilo,* named for a waterfall on the Columbia River. Charles R. McCormick had her built away back in 1913, to augment the fleet of steam schooners already engaged in hauling lumber from the McCormick mills on the Columbia to California ports. Many of the coastal towns were isolated even in that fairly recent year and had to depend largely upon water transportation; the *Celilo* was therefore fitted out to carry sixty passengers. Now, to accommodate sixty passengers, a crew of twenty, a million feet of lumber, a jag of general cargo, and now and then some livestock on the hoof, all in a ship only two hundred feet long, is something; the *Celilo* was a credit to the reputation of the naval architect who designed her. In appointments, the *Celilo* was years ahead of other steam schooners and small passenger craft; for one thing, she had running water in every stateroom, so you didn't have to wash in a bucket.

She's a relatively newcomer to the mudflats, is the *Celilo,* having been there only six years as this is written. Her owner has kept her in good shape, ready for anything that may turn up. And, as she is typical of the best in her class, let us make our way across the shaky plank to her silent deck and have a look around.

The captain's quarters are paneled in dark red hardwood, with a built-in bunk with drawers below, and across the cabin a settee. Square ports, draped with hop-sacking curtains, let in enough light to reveal dust on the pages of a years-old calendar. A brass lamp is secured to the bulkhead over the bunk, in just the right place for a reading light; even though the *Celilo* has electric lights, she kept up the tradition of shutting down the dynamo when she was in port.

There's an old-fashioned ship's clock over the desk, but it

isn't running now and has in fact been silent for years. On top of the desk is a litter of yellowing coastal charts and an empty frame which once held the master's certificate. A red rug, and an old easy chair complete the furnishings. All is silent—very silent indeed—and it is easy to let the imagination roll back the years and look once more on the long lines of seaman who filed into the cabin to sign on or to be paid off; also the passengers, who came up to pay their respects to the Old Man, and McCormick himself, who always kept in close touch with his captains and chief engineers.

An equally solemn spell is cast by the tiny social hall. An electric piano (badly out of tune, doubtless, and with several teeth missing) stands against a bulkhead, where passengers used to group themselves around this forerunner of the juke-box and sing, as the tiny ship made her way along the coast, "riding the breakers." A winding, twin companionway leads down into the dining saloon, where three long tables, with deck-secured chairs, accommodated thirty-eight passengers at one sitting.

What stories the old *Celilo* could tell! Vacationers traveling to San Francisco from the tiny mill towns; honeymooners, arm in arm, pacing the moonlit decks—and, yes, ladies of easy virtue (old women now) who not infrequently were passengers and whose presence in the steam schooners proved that they are not limited to the big liners. And there were days and nights of howling gales, when on more than one occasion the staunch little *Celilo* came to the aid of some storm-battered wind-jammer, being blown on the treacherous Mendocino coast.

The retirement of the *Celilo* may be attributed to the same cause as that of the other steam schooners—age, and changing conditions. McCormick sold her when he acquired steel ships and entered foreign fields. For a number of years she ran coastwise under another house-flag; but labor difficulties and increased operating costs led her owners to lay her up.

A gutted tug, the *Kadiak,* lies astern of the main fleet. She has been completely stripped of engines and boilers, and in the process of their removal even the crew's quarters have been torn away.

Little is known of her, other than that she was built nearly fifty years ago, not far from where her hulk lies today. Her name indicates Alaskan service; but no one in the vicinity can give her history.

For years a tall, four-masted schooner, the *William H. Smith,* rested with the little steamers, offering an interesting contrast in types. For a quarter of a century she carried lumber coastwise and to Australia, returning with cargoes of copra. Then she deserted the lumber business and for fifteen years was operated from San Francisco to the Bering Sea in the codfish trade. Her experiences in this service were varied; sailing to and from the banks, the fishermen worked her, and then, when they were "on fish," they turned to catching cod. Fish were taken by hook and line, from dories put over the side; "dressers" on board bled and cleaned the fish and stowed them below, and when she got back home the catch was processed by drying it on racks, in the Belvedere Island plant. South America and Mexico consumed most of her product. But now the *William H. Smith* is gone; some wartime job showed up in which she could be used. No one in the four corporations which operated her for years can identify the William H. Smith for whom she was named, and it is generally assumed that he was some early-day Puget Sound lumberman. Her most recent owner was an American Chinese, who kept her painted and in good shape.

In the winter of 1942 a bad sou'easter lashed at the little ships in Rotten Row; their lines carried away and they all were blown over on the north side of Oakland Creek, a sad jumble of old ships which must have thought, for the moment, that they were going to sea again. Tugs recaptured the vagrant vessels and returned them to the Alameda side of the channel, where a survey showed only superficial damage—mainly the loss of a few rails.

The few old skippers who are retained to stand watch over the idle craft wash down the decks, often enough to keep them relatively tight, and putter around on the broken gear. As a boom gives way it is painstakingly tossed over the side, as if to

127

hide the fact that, little by little, the old ships are falling apart. Electric power is secured from shoreside, and portable pumps keep the bilges dry—or, at least, comfortably low.

From time to time the lonely watchers of the forgotten fleet received visitors, either old coastwise mariners or laymen interested in things nautical. Then dust would be wiped away from the square ports of the vacant cabins, and tall yarns of the mudflat officers would bridge the years which have passed. But wartime security has made it necessary to keep casual callers away from these ships, which adjoin important industrial plants. An ugly sign, prominently displayed near the gangway, spells loneliness for the veteran mariners aboard—"NO VISITORS!"

The old captains have become reconciled to the fact that they are alone—that they, like the ships they guard, have been forgotten, replaced by newer ships and younger men. Perhaps they are content—content to sit and smoke their pipes, seeing in the ascending clouds of tobacco smoke the fogs of Mendocino, and the crested gray seas as the staunch little ship stood out of some now forgotten dog-hole, deckload chained down and scuppers spouting white froth.

And now a gray wall of fog shuts down on Rotten Row; masts and rigging become spectral shapes and the once brightly gold-leafed names—*Svea, Idaho, Celilo*—are blurred. In a few years they will be gone; but their memories and the memories of the lusty, hell-roaring mariners who sailed them will long remain.

APPENDIX

A. WOODEN STEAM SCHOONERS*

ABBREVIATIONS

A—Abandoned   B—Broken up   C—Collision   F—Lost by fire
Fo—Foundered   L—Laid up   Sa—Sold alien   St—Stranded

KEY TO BUILDERS

Abdn—Aberdeen Shipbuilding Co.
B&B—Boole & Beaton
B&W—Blanchard & Wheeler
Bdxn—Hans D. Bendixsen
Blrd—Ballard Shipbuilding Co.
Chris—C. Christensen
Dick—John W. Dickie
DikB—Dickie Brothers
Fult—Fulton Iron Works
Grays—Grays Harbor Shipbuilding Co.
GSP—Grant, Smith, Porter
GWB—George W. Boole
H&F—Hansen & Fraser
H&W—Hay & Wright
Hall—Hall Brothers
Hamm—Hammond Lumber Co.
Hay—Hay Shipbuilding Co.
Heuk—E. Heuckendorff
Hins—Hinsdale
Hitch—G. H. Hitchings
K&B—Kruse & Banks
Lind—John Lindstrom

McDa—John McDade
McEa—McEachern Shipbuilding Co.
Matt—Matthews Shipbuilding Co.
Pete—Andrew Peterson
Poll—Pollard Lumber Co.
Pri—J. H. Price
Reed—Reed Shipbuilding Co.
Rolf—Rolph Shipbuilding Co.
Ross—G. Ross
S&V—Stone & Van Bergen
St.H.—St. Helens Shipbuilding Co.
Smpsn—Simpson Lumber Co.
Stan—G. M. Standifer Corporation
Stone—W. G. Stone
Turn—Mathew Turner
Wash—Washington Marine Co.
WAB—William A. Boole
Whit—Charles G. White
Whtlw—Thomas Patrick Henry White-
      law
Will—Wilmington Shipbuilding Co.
Wlsn—Wilson Brothers

Name	Gross Tons	Builder	Where Built	When Built	Disposal and Date
Aberdeen	499	Lind	Aberdeen, Wash.	1899	St, San Francisco Bar, Jan. 23, 1916
Acme	416	Dick	Alameda, Calif.	1901	St. Coquille, Ore., Oct. 31, 1924

* Vessels propelled by other than steam, viz., by Diesel or auxiliary gasoline engines, have been omitted.

129

Name	Gross Tons	Builder	Where Built	When Built	Disposal and Date
Albion	214	H&W	Alameda, Calif.	1892	St, Stewart's Point, March 21, 1913
Albion River	382	....	....	....	St, Bodega
Alcatraz	255	Whit	San Francisco	1887	St, Greenwood, May 2, 1917
Alcazar	263	....	....	....	St, Needle Rock, June 10, 1907
Alex Duncan	...	....	San Francisco	....	....
Alice Blanchard[1]	393	B&W	Tacoma, Wash.	1890	St, Shelter Cove, July 18, 1906
Alliance	679	Bdxn	Fairhaven, Calif.	1896	Sa, Mexican
A. M. Simpson[2]	744	K&B	North Bend, Ore.	1911	B; hull a fish barge
Anne Hanify	1,343	K&B	North Bend, Ore.	1920	In operation 1943
Annette Rolph[3]	2,361	Rolf	Rolph, Calif.	1918	B, 1944
Arcata	560	DikB	San Francisco	1876	A, Oakland Creek, Calif.
Arctic	392	Whit	Bay City, Ore.	1901	St, Point Arena, July 5, 1922
Argo	210	....	Ballard, Wash.	1898	....
Aurelia	424	Ross	Prosper, Ore.	1902	Sa, 1920
Avalon	881	Matt	Hoquiam, Wash.	1912	St, Cape Shoalwater, April 29, 1925
Bandon	642	K&B	North Bend, Ore.	1907	St and L, Bandon, Ore.
Beda	...	....	....	1882	....
Bee	601	Lind	Aberdeen, Wash.	1904	St and L, Oakland Creek, Calif.
Bee	662	Lind	Aberdeen, Wash.	1907	St, Hawaiian waters
Berkeley	571	Lind	Aberdeen, Wash.	1906	F, Point Conception, Nov. 14, 1907
Bowdoin	756	Heuk	Prosper, Ore.	1907	Sold, East Coast, 1917
Brookdale	2,935	Grays	Grays Harbor	1918	B; converted to barge
Brooklyn	333	Lind	Aberdeen, Wash.	1901	Fo, Humboldt Bar, Nov. 8, 1930
Brunswick	512	Heuk	North Bend, Ore.	1898	In operation 1943
C. A. Smith	1,878	K&B	North Bend, Ore.	1921	St, Coos Bay, Dec. 16, 1923
Capistrano[4]	648	Lind	Aberdeen, Wash.	1907	B, 1941; made into barge
Carlos	865	S&V	San Francisco	1908	B, 1938; breakwater, San Pablo
Carmel	633	Lind	Aberdeen, Wash.	1906	B, 1931
Cascade	...	Bdxn	Fairhaven, Calif.	1904	Sa, Hawaiian, 1906
Casco	533	K&B	Marshfield, Ore.	1906	St, Piedras Blancas, 1913

[1] Renamed *Chico*.   [2] Renamed *Martha Buehner*.
[3] Renamed *Arthur J. Baldwin*, then *Bering*.   [4] Renamed *Caspar*.

Appendix

Name	Gross Tons	Builder	Where Built	When Built	Disposal and Date
Caspar	300	H&F	San Francisco	1887	St, Sanders Reef, 1897
Celia	173	Turn	San Francisco	1884	St, Monterey, 1906
Celilo	943	St.H	St. Helens, Ore.	1913	L, Oakland Creek
Centralia	487	Dick	Alameda, Calif.	1902	B; converted to barge
C. G. White.....	169	....	San Francisco	1884	....
Charles Nelson ..	629	H&W	Alameda, Calif.	1898	Fo, 1913; converted to barge
Chehalis	633	Bdxn	Fairhaven, Calif.	1901	A, Oakland Creek
Chilkat	215	....	Astoria, Ore.	....	St, Humboldt, April 2, 1899
C. H. Wheeler...	371	....	Portland, Ore.	1900	....
Claremont	747	Lind	Aberdeen, Wash.	1907	St, Coos Bay, 1915
Claremont[5]	1,291	Matt	Hoquiam, Wash.	1917	In operation 1943
Cleone	197	B&B	San Francisco	1887	....
Coaster[6]	579	Lind	Aberdeen, Wash.	1905	Fo, Columbia River, Feb. 5, 1925
Coos Bay	....	....	....	Fo, Ventura, Dec. 18, 1914
Coquille River ...	415	Chris	Prosper, Ore.	1896	A, Oakland Creek
Cornell[7]	837	Hall	Winslow, Wash.	1905	St, Cypress Point, Sept. 2, 1934
Coronado	578	Poll	Aberdeen, Wash.	1900	Fo, Point Arena, April 27, 1917
Cosmopolis	339	B&B	San Francisco	1887	Sa, Hawaiian
Crescent City	...	....	.. ..	....	St, Fish Rock, Jan. 30, 1903
Daisy	621	....	Fair Harbor, Ore.	1907	....
Daisy[8]	679	Pri	Bandon, Ore.	1908	F, Humboldt Bay, Sept. 18, 1939
Daisy Freeman ...	613	Bdxn	Fairhaven, Calit.	1908	B, Oakland Creek
Daisy Gadsby	818	Matt	Hoquiam, Wash.	1911	In operation 1943
Daisy Gray	1,187	Matt	Portland, Ore.	1923	In operation 1943
Daisy Matthews ..	943	Matt	Hoquiam, Wash.	1916	Fo, Trinidad Head, 1940
Daisy Mitchell[9]...	612	Bdxn	Fairhaven, Calif.	1905	....
Daisy Putnam	886	Matt	Hoquiam, Wash.	1913	St, Punta Gorda, Nov. 22, 1920
Davenport	91ʳ	K&B	North Bend, Ore.	1912	In operation 1943
David C. Meyer..	2,510	McEa	Astoria, Ore.	1920	St, San Pedro, 1926
Delhi	968	Hall	Winslow, Wash.	1906	St, Alaska, Jan. 20, 1915
Del Norte	450	B&B	San Francisco	1890	....
Del Norte	301	Dick	Tiburon, Calif.	1890	St, Point Arena, July 27, 1917

[5] Renamed *Alwill*, then *North Bend*.   [6] Renamed *Caoba*.
[7] Renamed *J. B. Stetson*.   [8] Renamed *Thomas H. Elliot*, then *Redwood*.
[9] Renamed *La Primera*.

Name	Gross Tons	Builder	Where Built	When Built	Disposal and Date
Despatch	698	Bdxn	Fairhaven, Calif.	1899	Sa, Alaskan
Doris	725	Dick	Raymond, Wash.	1908	B, 1925
Egeria[10]	2,360	Wlsn	Astoria, Ore.	1920	....
Elizabeth	363	S&V	San Francisco	1903	Sa, Mexican
Emily	285	Whit	San Francisco	1887	....
Empire	....	....	....	Sa; used as gunboat
Ernest H. Meyer..1,057		St.H	St. Helens, Ore.	1917	B, 1930
Esther Johnson...1,104		Matt	Portland, Ore.	1923	In operation 1943
Everett 1,751		St.H	St. Helens, Ore.	1920	F, Table Bluff, 1926
Excelsior	526	Matt	Eureka, Calif.	1893	C, San Francisco, 1916
Fairhaven	751	K&B	North Bend, Ore.	1908	Fo, Mexico, March 19, 1922
Farallons	368	Hay	San Francisco	1888	....
Fifield	634	K&B	North Bend, Ore.	1908	St, Coquille River, 1916
Flavel	967	McDa	Eureka, Calif.	1917	Fo, Monterey, June 1925
Forest King 2,426		GSP	Aberdeen, Wash.	1919	Fo, Mexico, 1940
Fort Bragg	705	Pri	Fairhaven, Calif.	1910	St, Coos Bay, Sept. 7, 1932
Frank D. Stout[11] 1,113		St.H.	St. Helens, Ore.	1917	St, Port Orford, 1937
Fred Baxter......1,294		K&B	North Bend, Ore.	1917	B
F. S. Loop......	794	K&B	Marshfield, Ore.	1907	Sa, Mexican; used as barge
Fulton	380	Bdxn	Fairhaven, Calif.	1898	Sa, Puget Sound
G. C. Lindauer....453		Lind	Aberdeen, Wash.	1901	St, Umpqua River, May 16, 1924
Georgina Rolph..2,361		Rolf	Rolph, Calif.	1918	B, 1930's
Grays Harbor	659	Lind	Aberdeen, Wash.	1907	B
Graywood[12]	915	Bdxn	Fairhaven, Calif.	1904	Fo, Umpqua River, Oct. 2, 1915
Greenwood	192	Whtlw	San Francisco	1886	A, Oakland Creek
Gualala[13]	228	Dick	Alameda, Calif.	1901	St, Blunts Reef, 1931
Halco	870	McDa	Fairhaven, Calif.	1918	St, Grays Harbor, 1925
Hanalei	666	H&W	Alameda, Calif.	1901	St, Bolinas, Nov. 23, 1914
Hardy[14]	429	Fult	San Francisco	1898	....
Hartwood	946	Matt	Hoquiam, Wash.	1916	St, Point Reyes, June 27, 1929
H. B. Lovejoy....1,067		Blrd	Seattle, Wash.	1918	B; breakwater, San Pablo Bay
Helene	672	Matt	Hoquiam, Wash.	1906	Fo, Richardson Bay
Helen P. Drew...	309	Hitch	Hoquiam, Wash.	1904	L, Martinez, Calif.
Homer	331	Reed	Bandon, Ore.	1891	B; used as barge

[10] Renamed *Bert E. Haney.* [11] Renamed *Cottoneva.*

[12] Ex-*Harold Dollar.* [13] Renamed *Cleone.*

[14] Renamed *Grace Dollar*, then *San Antonio.*

Appendix

Name	Gross Tons	Builder	Where Built	When Built	Disposal and Date
Hoquiam	644	Bdxn	Fairhaven, Calif.	1906	St, Salinas Cruz, Feb. 8, 1944
Hueneme[15]	...	Bdxn	Fairhaven, Calif.	1897	Sa, Hawaiian; A, 1928
H. X. Baxter[16]	1,293	K&B	North Bend, Ore.	1917	In operation 1943
Iaqua	712	Bdxn	Fairhaven, Calif.	1900	Sold, East Coast
Idaho	1,047	Pete	Aberdeen, Wash.	1917	L, Oakland Creek
Jane Nettleton	1,545	Will	San Pedro, Calif.	1917	B; hull at San Pablo
Jewel	265	Hay	San Francisco	1888	....
Jim Butler[17]	701	Lind	Aberdeen, Wash.	1906	St, Fish Rock
J. J. Loggie	404	Pri	Bandon, Ore.	1908	St, Point Arguello, Oct. 1912
J. Marhoffer	608	Lind	Aberdeen, Wash.	1907	St, off Oregon, 1910
Johanna Smith	1,921	K&B	North Bend, Ore.	1917	Gambling barge
Johan Poulson	650	Whit	Everett, Wash.	1905	Fo, 1938
J. S. Higgins	392	Lind	Aberdeen, Wash.	1904	St, Albion, Dec. 23, 1919
Julia H. Ray	177	....	San Francisco	1889	St, Coos Bay, 1885
Katherine	531	Lind	Fairhaven, Calif.	1908	B, 1940
K. Donovan[18]	993	K&B	North Bend, Ore.	1913	St, Humboldt Bay, Jan. 22, 1941
Klamath	1,038	Pri	Fairhaven, Calif.	1910	St, Del Mar Landing, Feb. 5, 1921
Laguna	185	B&B	San Francisco	1885	....
Lakme	529	Hins	Pt. Madison, Wash.	1888	A, Oakland Creek
Lassen	717	Matt	Hoquiam, Wash.	1917	B; hull at Sausalito
Libbey-Maine	1,811	Stan	Portland, Ore.	1918	Fo, Mexico, Sept. 16, 1941
Lucinda Hanify	1,482	Will	Wilmington, Calif.	1917	B, 1937
Luella	412	....	Florence, Ore.	1898	....
Majestic	810	....	San Francisco	1908	Fo, Point Sur, 1909
Mandalay	438	Smpsn	North Bend, Ore.	1900	St, Crescent City, Oct. 8, 1918
Marshfield[19]	409	Heuk	Marshfield, Ore.	1901	....
Mary Olson	844	Hamm	Eureka, Calif.	1913	F, Cuba
Mayfair	670	Lind	Aberdeen, Wash.	1905	B, 1936; hull in Oakland Creek
Mendocino	251	Hay	San Francisco	1888	....
Merced	969	St.H	St. Helens, Ore.	1912	St, Punta Gorda, Oct. 15, 1913
Michigan	566	....	Shamokawa, Wash.	1888	St, Vancouver Island, 1893
Mukilteo	1,230	Pete	Raymond, Wash.	1915	F, Antioch
Multnomah	969	St.H	St. Helens, Ore.	1913	F and B, St. Helens, Ore.
National City	310	H&W	San Francisco	1888	Sa, Peru, 1918

[15] Renamed Nihau. [16] Renamed Port Orford. [17] Renamed Crescent City.
[18] Ex-San Ramon. [19] Renamed Bertie M. Hanlon.

133

Name	Gross Tons	Builder	Where Built	When Built	Disposal and Date
Navarro	232	H&W	San Francisco	1887	....
Necanicum	752	Hamm	Fairhaven, Calif.	1912	Fo, San Pablo Bay, 1936
Nehalem	632	Hamm	Fairhaven, Calif.	1910	B, 1937
Newberg	450	Dick	San Francisco	1898	St, Bodega, Oct. 8, 1918
Newport	247	DikB	San Francisco	1875	....
Newsboy	208	B&B	San Francisco	1888	C with *Wasp*, Humboldt, 1906
Nome City	939	Bdxn	Fairhaven, Calif.	1900	F, Antioch
North Fork	322	Bdxn	Fairhaven, Calif.	1888	St, Punta Gorda, Sept. 12, 1919
Northland	845	Bdxn	Fairhaven, Calif.	1904	C, San Francisco Bay, 1927
Norwood	760	Hall	Winslow, Wash.	1904	B, 1933
Noyo	316	H&W	San Francisco	1888	....
Olympic	688	Hitch	Hoquiam, Wash.	1901	....
O. M. Clark[20]	844	Matt	Hoquiam, Wash.	1913	Fo, Oct. 27, 1918
Oregon	989	Pete	Aberdeen, Wash.	1916	L, Oakland Creek
Pacific[21]	1,240	K&B	North Bend, Ore.	1920	In operation 1943
Pasadena	300	H&W	San Francisco	1887	A, Oakland Creek
Phoenix[22]	256	H&W	Alameda, Calif.	1902	A, Oakland Creek
Phyllis	1,266	Abdn	Aberdeen, Wash.	1917	St, Port Orford, 1935
Point Arena	223	GWB	San Francisco	1887	St, Pigeon Point, Aug. 9, 1913
Pomo	368	Bdxn	Fairhaven, Calif.	1903	Fo and F, Drakes Bay, Jan. 1, 1913
Port Angeles	1,358	K&B	North Bend, Ore.	1917	Sa, Russia; B, Antioch, 1937
Prentiss	406	WAB	Oakland, Calif.	1902	B, San Pedro, 1935
Protection	281	H&F	San Francisco	1888	....
Quinault	582	Lind	Aberdeen, Wash.	1906	St, Punta Gorda, Oct. 4, 1917
Quinault	1,138	Matt	Portland, Ore.	1921	In operation 1943
Rainier	800	Hitch	Hoquiam, Wash.	1900	....
Ravalli	998	Bdxn	Fairhaven, Calif.	1905	F, Alaskan waters, 1918
Raymond	595	Heuk	Prosper, Ore.	1906	B, 1931
R. D. Inman	717	K&B	North Bend, Ore.	1907	St, San Francisco Bar, 1909
Redwood City[23]	258	Dick	Alameda, Calif.	1901	Fo, San Francisco, 1943
Rival	266	....	San Francisco	1888	A, Oakland Creek
Robert Dollar[24]	798	Hitch	Hoquiam, Wash.	1900	Sold, East Coast, 1917
Rochelle	632	S&B	Michigan (rebuilt)	1896	....
Rosalie Mahoney[25]	844	Matt	Hoquiam, Wash.	1913	....
Ruth	377	....	San Francisco	1898	St, 1903
Ryder Hanify[26]	1,428	Stone	Oakland, Calif.	1917	St, Coos Bay, 1944

[20] Renamed *Willie A. Higgins*. [21] Renamed *Barbara C.* [22] Renamed *Aloha*.
[23] Ex-*Unimak*, then *Redwood City*, then *Manuel Espinosa*. [24] Renamed *Fair Oaks*.
[25] Renamed *Border Queen*. [26] Renamed *Gabriel*, then *George L. Olson*.

Appendix

Name	Gross Tons	Builder	Where Built	When Built	Disposal and Date
Ryder Hanify	1,342	K&B	North Bend, Ore.	1920	In operation 1943
Saginaw	886	Matt	Hoquiam, Wash.	1907	B, 1940
Samoa	377	Dick	San Francisco	1898	St, Point Reyes, Jan. 28, 1913
San Diego	1,487	Matt	Portland, Ore.	1918	L, Oakland Creek
San Jacinto[27]	614	Matt	Hoquiam, Wash.	1908	St, Cuba, 1944
San Pedro	456	Lind	Aberdeen, Wash.	1899	Sa, 1920
Santa Ana	1,203	Reed	Marshfield, Ore.	1900	B, 1940
Santa Barbara	695	Stone	San Francisco	1900	B, 1943; hull in breakwater, San Francisco Bay
Santa Monica	497	Stone	San Francisco	1902	In operation 1943
Santiam	946	McDa	Fairhaven, Calif.	1916	F, Aberdeen, Wash., 1936
Scotia	181	H&W	San Francisco	1888	St, Purisima Point, July 28, 1914
Sea Foam	339	Lind	Aberdeen, Wash.	1904	St, Point Arena, Feb. 23, 1931
Shasta	722	Hitch	Hoquiam, Wash.	1903	St, Point Conception, 1906
Shasta	878	Matt	Hoquiam, Wash.	1908	B, 1933; hull whaling barge
Shna Yak[28]	839	Hall	Winslow, Wash.	1907	B, 1936; hull at San Pablo
Shoshone[29]	646	Bdxn	Fairhaven, Calif.	1908	Sa, Hawaiian
Sibyl Marston	1,086	WAB	San Francisco	....	St, Surf, Calif., 1909
Signal	475	Fult	San Francisco	1887	Fo, San Francisco, 1911
Silver Spring	245	....	San Francisco	1888	....
Siskiyou	884	Matt	Aberdeen, Wash.	1912	B; hull at San Pablo Bay
Solano	943	Pete	North Bend, Ore.	1913	In operation 1943
South Bay	438	....	Tacoma, Wash.	1901	Fo, Mexico, 1917
South Coast	301	Whit	Seattle, Wash.	1887	Fo, Oregon, 1931
Speedwell	914	K&B	North Bend, Ore.	1912	Sold, East Coast
Stanwood	1,129	K&B	Portland, Ore.	1916	In operation 1943
Sunol	258	....	Alameda, Calif.	1890	F, Little River, Oct. 23, 1900
Surprise	165	Whit	San Francisco	1884	....
Svea	618	Bdxn	Fairhaven, Calif.	1906	L, Oakland Creek
Tahoe	751	Lind	Hoquiam, Wash.	1907	Sa, Panama, 1943
Tamalpais	574	Matt	Hoquiam, Wash.	1906	B, 1931
Temple E. Dorr	720	Matt	Hoquiam, Wash.	1907	F, Cuba, 1919
Thomas L. Wand	657	Lind	Aberdeen, Wash.	1906	St, Point Sur, Sept. 16, 1933
Tillamook	265	GWB	San Francisco	1887	....

[27] Renamed *Border King*.
[28] Renamed *Charles Christensen*.
[29] Renamed *Hamakua*.

Name	Gross Tons	Builder	Where Built	When Built	Disposal and Date
Tiverton	557	Hitch	Hoquiam, Wash.	1906	St, Humboldt Bay, March 13, 1933
Trinidad	974	Hamm	Fairhaven, Calif.	1918	St, Willapa Bay, May 7, 1937
Unimak[30]	258	Dick	Alameda, Calif.	1901	Fo, San Francisco, 1943
Vanguard	358	Dick	Alameda, Calif.	1904	In operation 1943
Venture	249	Hay	San Francisco	1888	St, Rockport, 1892
Viking 1,210		Rolf	Rolph, Calif.	1920	Fo, Alaskan waters, 1944
Wahkeena 1,030		Wlsn	Astoria, Ore.	1917	St, Grays Harbor, 1929
Wapama[31]	951	St.H	St. Helens, Ore.	1915	In operation 1943
Washington	539	Wash	Seattle, Wash.	1906	F and B, Humboldt Bay, Feb. 15, 1932
Wasp	563	Pri	Fairhaven, Calif.	1905	F, Pensacola, June 19, 1919
Wellesley	709	Heuk	Prosper, Ore.	1907	B, 1943; hull at Sausalito
Weott	249	....	Alameda, Calif.	1893	St, Humboldt Bar, 1899
West Coast	179	Whit	San Francisco	1885	....
Westport	211	GWB	San Francisco	1888	A, Oakland Creek, 1930's
Whitesboro	195	Whit	San Francisco	1886	A, Oakland Creek
Whitney Olson[32]	1,558	Will	San Pedro, Calif.	1917	In operation 1943
W. H. Kreuger...	469	Lind	Aberdeen, Wash.	1899	Fo, Point Arena, 1906
W. H. Murphy..	923	Matt	Hoquiam, Wash.	1907	F, Trinidad, 1918
Willamette[33]	903	Bdxn	Fairhaven, Calif.	1911	Fo, Crescent City, 1942
Willapa	752	K&B	North Bend, Ore.	1908	Sold, East Coast
Willapa[34] 1,185		K&B	North Bend, Ore.	1917	Fo, Port Orford, 1941
Wilmington	990	K&B	Prosper, Ore.	1913	Fo, Humboldt Bar
Yellowstone	767	Bdxn	Fairhaven, Calif.	1907	Fo, Humboldt Bay, Feb. 24, 1933
Yosemite	827	Bdxn	Fairhaven, Calif.	1906	St, Point Reyes, Feb. 23, 1936

[30] Renamed *Redwood City*, then *Manuel Espinosa*.   [31] Renamed *Tongass*.

[32] Ex-*Ghislaine*, then *Edna Christensen*.

[33] Renamed *California*, then *Susan Olson*.   [34] Ex-*Florence Olson*.

B. STEAM-SCHOONER CONVERSIONS

Steam Schooner	Use to Which Converted
Aberdeen	Garbage ship
Bee	Cattle carrier
Bertie M. Hanlon[1]	Fish-reduction ship
Cascade	Cattle carrier
Centralia	Fish-reduction ship
Chehalis	Salvage ship
Cleone	Gasoline tank ship
Empire	Gunboat
F. S. Loop	Fish-reduction ship
Fair Oaks[2]	Dredge
Greenwood	Wrecking ship
Helen P. Drew	Fish-reduction ship
Homer	Salvage ship
Hoquiam	Garbage ship
Iaqua	Wrecking ship
Johan Poulson	Gambling barge
Lassen	Fish-reduction ship
Martha Buehner[3]	Fish-reduction ship
Pasadena	Salvage tender (oil skimmer)
Prentiss	Barge
Shoshone	Cattle carrier
Signal	Garbage ship
Tahoe	Garbage ship
Unimak	Ammunition carrier

[1] Ex-Marshfield.   [2] Ex-Robert Dollar.   [3] Ex-A. M. Simpson.

C. STEAM-SCHOONER OPERATORS

Albion Lumber Company
Atlas Steamship Company
Andrews, N.
Baxter, J. H.
Beadle, Alfred W.
Beadle & Antz Steamship Co.
Beadle, Donald
Beadle, George S.
Billings, G. E.
Borderline Transportation Co.
Byxbee & Clark
California-Oregon Lumber Co.
Caspar Lumber Company
Chamberlin, W. R.
Cottoneva Lumber Company
Coos Bay Lumber Company
Davenport, J. E.
Davenport, J. O.
Dodge, E. H.
Dodge, E. J.
Doe, Charles P.
Dolbeer & Carson
Dollar, Robert
Donovan Lumber Company
Eastern Redwood Lumber Co.
Estabrook, A. F.
Excelsior Lumber Company
Forest King Company
Foster, Charles
Freeman Steamship Company
Fritch, J. Homer
Goodyear Redwood Lumber Company
Gray & Holt
Hammond Lumber Company
Hanify Lumber Company
Hardy Steamship Company
Hart-Wood Lumber Company
Hicks-Hauptmann Lumber Co.
Higgins, Charles H.
Hobbs, Wall & Company
Hubbard, Russell S.
Independent Steamship Co.
Johnson, A. B.
Kimball, J. S.
Kruse, E. T.
Langley, Wallace
Linderman, Fred

Little River Steamship Co.
Loop Lumber Company
MacKay Lumber Company
McCormick Steamship Company
McCullough Steamship Company
McPherson, Frank C.
Mahoney, Andrew F.
Mason, J. V.
Merchants Steamship Company
Metropolitan Redwood Lumber Co.
Milford Lumber Company
Moore Mill & Lumber Company
National Steamship Company
Nelson Steamship Company
Northwestern Shipping Company
Ogden, John
Oliver J. Olson Company
Olson & Mahoney Steamship Co.
Oregon Marine Company
P & L Transportation Co.
Pacific Coast Steamship Company
Pollard Steamship Company
Pope & Talbot Lumber Company
Ramselius, J.
Redwood Steamship Company
Richardson, H. A.
Rogers, W. J.
Rolph Navigation Company
Santa Cruz–Monterey SS. Co.
Scammell, W. S.
Signal Steamship Company
Simpson Lumber Company
Slade, S. E.
South Coast Steamship Company
Sudden & Christensen Company
Sudden & Heitman Lumber Co.
Sudden, Robert C.
Swayne & Hoyt Steamship Co.
Templeton, Henry
Tibbitts, W. G.
Trower Brothers
Union Lumber Company
Wendling, G. E.
White, Lorenzo E.
Wilson Brothers
Wilson & Fyfe
Wood, E. K.

Appendix

D. LUMBER PORTS OF NORTHERN CALIFORNIA

	Nautical Miles from San Francisco		Nautical Miles from San Francisco
Albion	117	Iversen's Landing	91
Arcata	215	Laguna	132
Arena Cove	95	Little River	120
Bear Harbor	158	Mad River	219
Big River	121	Mattole Landing	182
Black Point Landing	81	Monroe Landing	153
Bodega	58	Moss Landing	72
Bowen's Landing	87	Navarro Landing	115
Caspar	125	Needle Rock	159
Cleone	132	Noyo Anchorage	128
Crescent City	278	Requa	256
Cuffey Cove	111	Rockport	147
Davenport Landing	52	Rollerville	108
Del Mar Landing	84	Rolph (Fairhaven)	215
Duncan Landing	64	Russian Gulch	123
Eel River	202	Salt Point Landing	74
Eureka	221	Samoa	216
Fairhaven (Rolph)	215	Shelter Cove	164
Field's Landing	222	Smith River	289
Fish Rock	88	Stewart's Point	79
Fisk Mill Cove	76	Trinidad	226
Fort Bragg	129	Usal	153
Fort Ross	71	Union Landing	143
Greenwood	110	Walsh's Landing	74
Gualala	86	Westport	141
Hardy Creek	146	Whitesboro	116
Humboldt Bay	214		

E. MASTERS OF THE WOODEN STEAMERS

The following roster of wooden steam-schooner skippers has been compiled from daily shipping notices and old newspaper files. No attempt has been made to obtain given names of the masters and for that reason complete identification of ship and master has not been possible. One must bear in mind that there was many a change-over in the steam-schooner field, both in ship ownership and in command. Also many of the names included herein were probably relief skippers, taking the run for the regular master, who may have been on vacation. The list has been restricted to wooden steam-schooner masters.

Surname of Captain	Vessels Commanded and Years

Abbors ....*Wapama*, 1935–1936; *Celilo*, 1935

Adler ....*Newsboy*, 1904

Ahlin[1] ....*Casco*, 1908; *Marshfield*, 1912, 1914; *Solano*, 1919; *Tamalpais*, 1924, 1927, 1930; *Washington*, 1919, 1927, 1928–1931; *Tiverton*, 1931–1932; *Brunswick*, 1932–1933

Ahlstrom ....*Prentiss*, 1904; *Aberdeen*, 1906; *Daisy Freeman*, 1927

Alexander ......*Santa Barbara*, 1904

Allen ....*Del Norte*, 1899–1900; *G. C. Lindauer*, 1904–1906; *Svea*, 1907–1909

Anderson[2] ......*Navarro*, 1887–1888; *Laguna*, 1888; *Chilkat*, 1899; *Charles Nelson*, 1900; *Prentiss*, 1904; *South Bay*, 1906; *Helene*, 1908; *Tamalpais*, 1908; *Centralia*, 1915; *Norwood*, 1919; *Helene*, 1919; *Willapa*, 1926–1927; *Claremont*, 1929; *Carlos*, 1930; *Stanwood*, 1932; *F. S. Loop*, 1935–1936; *Katherine Donovan*, 1937; *Esther Johnson*, 1942; *Ryder Hanify*, 1942.

Andresen ......*Brunswick*, 1899–1900

Anfindson ......*Willapa*, 1908; *Temple E. Dorr*, 1912

Arneson ....*Everett*, 1936

Arnke ....*Hartwood*, 1927

Arntsen ....*Phyllis*, 1919

Asplund ....*Shoshone*, 1908–1912

Baach ....*Helen P. Drew*, 1919; *Prentiss*, 1926–1931; *Martha Buehner*, 1930

Bachman ......*Daisy Gray*, 1929–1942

Badger ....*Atlas*, 1906–1908

Banke ....*Siskiyou*, 1927; *Barbara C*, 1930–1942

Bash ....*North Fork*, 1898–1899; *Iaqua*, 1900–1901

Baughman ......*Humboldt*, 1904–1930; *Celilo*, 1931–1933

Baye ....*J. B. Stetson*, 1926

Beck ....*Pasadena*, 1919–1928 (supposedly on the *Pasadena* from 1898 to 1928)

Beach ....*Marshfield*, 1915

Bellesen ....*J. B. Stetson*, 1915; *Wahkeena*, 1919

Bendegard ......*Signal*, 1888–1900

[1] Three Ahlins skippered steam schooners; believed to be father and two sons.

[2] Lack of information on given names prevents proper identification of master and vessel commanded.

Appendix

Surname of Captain	Vessels Commanded and Years
Bender	*Phyllis,* 1919
Benedikten	*Nehalem,* 1915
Bergersen	*Phoenix,* 1919
Bergmark	*Katherine,* 1926–1931; *Brunswick,* 1937
Bliesath	*Quinault,* 1942
Bodge	*Northland,* 1912
Boese	*Laguna,* 1887
Bonifield	*J. B. Stetson,* 1908
Bostrom	*Arctic,* 1908; *National City,* 1912–1914; *Coquille River,* 1919
Bowen	*Coos Bay,* 1914; *Daisy Freeman,* 1915
Bray	*Surprise,* 1900
Brix	*North Bend,* 1927
Burtis	*Weott,* 1899
Butler	*Empire,* 1884–1887
Butzing	*Westport,* 1919; *Saginaw,* 1927; *Sea Foam,* 1928; *Daisy,* 1931–1932; *Siskiyou,* 1933
Carey	*Aberdeen,* 1908
Carlsen	*Centralia,* 1912; *Whitney Olson,* 1937
Carlson	*Alcatraz,* 1898–1901; *Brooklyn,* 1904; *Yellowstone,* 1919; *Daisy Matthews,* 1930–1933
Carson	*Willamette,* 1929
Clark	*Brunswick,* 1942
Clemensen	*Stanwood,* 1936–1942
Cousins	*Ravalli,* 1906
Dahlquist	*Lakme,* 1909; *Nome City,* 1914; *Port Angeles,* 1919
Danielson	*Anne Hanify,* 1942
Danskanen	*Ernest H. Meyer,* 1919
Darwin	*Greenwood,* 1906
Denny	*Coos Bay,* 1885
Dettmers	*Celia,* 1884–1887; *Cosmopolis,* 1887–1888; *Sunol,* 1898; *National City,* 1900–1901; *Marshfield,* 1904–1906; *Tiverton,* 1912; *Katherine,* 1919
Devitt	*Daisy Gadsby,* 1915; *Daisy Putnam,* 1919
Dickson	*Pasadena,* 1904
Dodge	*Cleone,* 1888
Donaldson	*Homer,* 1904–1906; *Daisy,* 1929
Dunham	*Chilkat,* 1898; *Weott,* 1899
Eliason	*James S. Higgins,* 1915; *Jim Butler,* 1917
Ellefson	*Newsboy,* 1899; *Brunswick,* 1904–1906
Elleson	*Alcatraz,* 1908; *Fort Bragg,* 1912
Enstrom	*Hartwood,* 1929; *Quinault,* 1931
Erickson	*Greenwood,* 1887; *Noyo,* 1888; *Westport,* 1900; *Gualala,* 1900, 1906; *Albion,* 1901; *Aurelia,* 1904; *Centralia,* 1904–1906
Ericsson	*Laguna,* 1899–1900; *Greenwood,* 1887
Escher	*Point Arena,* 1887
Faarstran	*Yellowstone,* 1927
Fagerlund	*Greenwood,* 1898–1900; *Elizabeth,* 1913

Surname of Captain	Vessels Commanded and Years
Fagerstrom	*Point Arena*, 1912; *Bandon*, 1927–1928; *Cleone*, 1930; *Bandon*, 1930–1933
Faria	*Eureka*, 1914
Fegerstrad	*Alcazar*, 1907
Fletcher	*Redwood*, 1919
Foldat	*Multnomah*, 1915; *Wapama*, 1917
Fosen	*Newsboy*, 1900; *Rival*, 1904
Frederickson	*Whitesboro*, 1908, 1912; *Svea*, 1915, 1917; *Unimak*, 1919; *Westport*, 1926–1927; *South Coast*, 1929; *Ryder Hanify*, 1929; *Cleone*, 1930
Fredrickson	*Alcatraz*, 1906
Fridman	*Phoenix*, 1919
Gage	*Beda*, 1884
Generaux	*Laguna*, 1900
Gerdan	*Alcazar*, 1887
Gielow	*Coos Bay*, 1900
Graves	*Point Arena*, 1888; *Pasadena*, 1926; *Prentiss*, 1930
Green	*Sunol*, 1900
Gunderson	*Alcazar*, 1898–1900; *Charles Nelson*, 1904; *Helen P. Drew*, 1906, 1907, 1912; *Martha Buehner*, 1927–1928; *Esther Johnson*, 1932–1933
Hagan	*Brunswick*, 1929
Hall	*Coos Bay*, 1898; *Alice Blanchard*, 1899; *Delhi*, 1906, 1907
Halverson	*Rival*, 1906; *Katherine*, 1915; *Mayfair*, 1919; *Shasta*, 1926; *John C. Kirkpatrick*, 1927
Hamilton	*Pasadena*, 1888–1898
Hammer	*National City*, 1904; *Arctic*, 1908; *Coquille River*, 1909
Hammersten	*Svea*, 1919
Hana	*Nome City*, 1930
Hansen[3]	*Alcazar*, 1887; *Newberg*, 1899; *Point Arena*, 1900; *Rainier*, 1900; *H. B. Lovejoy*, 1901; *Aberdeen*, 1904; *Celia*, 1906; *Shasta*, 1906; *Argo*, 1907; *Phoenix*, 1907; *Tallac*, 1908; *Carlos*, 1913; *Girlie Mahoney*, 1919; *Chehalis*, 1919, 1927; *Santa Barbara*, 1924, 1926–1927
Hanson	*Point Arena*, 1898–1899; *Nome City*, 1908
Hardwick	*Alliance*, 1899–1904; *Carmel*, 1912
Harkins	*Coos Bay*, 1887
Hecker	*Phyllis*, 1930
Hellesten	*Brunswick*, 1927; *Santiam*, 1929
Hellesto	*Santiam*, 1930–1933; *Trinidad*, 1936
Hellestrom	*Noyo*, 1926
Hendricksen	*Newsboy*, 1900; *Phoenix*, 1904; *Brooklyn*, 1908; *Sea Foam*, 1912, 1915, 1926

[3] Lack of information on given names prevents proper identification of master and vessel commanded.

Appendix

~~~~~~

Surname of Captain	Vessels Commanded and Years

Higgins[4] ....*Silver Spring*, 1888; *South Coast*, 1888; *Aberdeen*, 1900; *Cleone*, 1899, 1900; *James S. Higgins*, 1906-1908; *National City*, 1908; *Caoba*, 1908; *Coaster*, 1912; *Navarro*, 1899

Holm ....*Lakme*, 1915; *Saginaw*, 1919

Holman ....*North Fork*, 1919; *Helene*, 1924

Holt ....*Arcata*, 1884

Hubner ....*F. S. Loop*, 1925; *J. B. Stetson*, 1927–1933; *Davenport*, 1942

Hughes ....*Tillamook*, 1900

Humphreys ....*Salinas*, 1887; *Jeanie*, 1888; *Excelsior*, 1900

Huntley ....*Phoenix*, 1915

Hutton ....*Shna Yak*, 1908; *Whitney Olson*, 1936

Iverson ....*Charles Nelson*, 1904; *Pasadena*, 1906; *Prentiss*, 1908, 1919

Jacobs ....*Westport*, 1888; *Scotia*, 1900; *Samoa*, 1900; *Navarro*, 1904; *Pomo*, 1904

Jacobsen ....*Noyo*, 1917; *Marshfield*, 1919; *Stanwood*, 1930; *Phyllis*, 1932–1935

Jaeger ....*Santiam*, 1936; *Ryder Hanify*, 1937

Jahnsen ....*Samoa*, 1898, 1899; *F. A. Kilburn*, 1904; *J. B. Stetson*, 1912; *Klamath*, 1912

Jamieson ....*South Bay*, 1904; *Northland*, 1904; *San Ramon*, 1915; *Klamath*, 1919, 1921; *Esther Johnson*, 1927, 1929

Jensen ....*Mendocino*, 1888; *Navarro*, 1900; *Elizabeth*, 1904, 1906; *Fifield*, 1908–1912; *Marshfield*, 1919; *Multnomah*, 1929

Jessen ....*Homer*, 1898; *Alice Blanchard*, 1900

Johannsen ......*Florence Olson*, 1927; *H. W. Baxter*, 1929; *Redwood*, 1936-1937

Johansen ....*Chehalis*, 1904, 1906; *Alcatraz*, 1912; *Helen P. Drew*, 1915; *Tiverton*, 1926–1927; *Wapama*, 1929; *Brooklyn*, 1930; *Whitney Olson*, 1942

Johnson[5] ....*Alcatraz*, 1887–1888; *Jewel*, 1888; *Greenwood*, 1888; *Scotia*, 1888; *Celia*, 1888, 1904; *Despatch*, 1900; *Rival*, 1899–1900; *Noyo*, 1899–1912; *Coquille River*, 1898; *Whitesboro*, 1898–1899; *Brooklyn*, 1904; *Coos Bay*, 1904; *Iaqua*, 1906; *Breakwater*, 1906; *Newsboy*, 1906; *Tiverton*, 1907–1919; *Daisy Freeman*, 1908; *Daisy Mitchell*, 1908; *Fair Oaks*, 1909; *Fairhaven*, 1913; *Celilo*, 1914; *Willapa*, 1915; *H. X. Baxter*, 1919; *Davenport*, 1919; *Raymond*, 1919; *Multnomah*, 1919; *Centralia*, 1926; *Willamette*, 1926; *Brooklyn*, 1929; *Wapama*, 1929–1931; *San Diego*, 1930–1931; *Trinidad*, 1933; *Quinault*, 1933; *George L. Olson*, 1937

Jorgenson ......*Aloha*, 1900; *Iaqua*, 1904; *Mayfair*, 1926

Justen ....*Scotia*, 1912; *Svea*, 1927

Kallsman ......*South Coast*, 1927

Kalnin ....*Pasadena*, 1908

Kelly ....*Westerner*, 1913

Kelvin ....*Unimak*, 1931

[4] There were three Captains Higgins—the father (J. S.) and two sons.

[5] There were several Johnsons: Rough-pile Johnson, Pie-face Johnson, Ving und Ving Yonson (he had large ears).

Surname of Captain   Vessels Commanded and Years

Kirkwood ......*Atlas*, 1915

Kittleson ....*Chehalis*, 1912; *Raymond*, 1914

Kjellen ....*Gualala*, 1907

Klinker ....*South Coast*, 1909

Klose ....*Shna Yak*, 1912–1915; *Tamalpais*, 1919

Knudsen ....*Carmel*, 1919

Koenig ....*National City*, 1888

Koffold ....*Saginaw*, 1912

Koteritz ....*Phoenix*, 1912

Krause ....*South Coast*, 1919–1926; *Elizabeth*, 1927–1935

Krog ....*Bee*, 1906

Landcaster .....*Johann Poulson*, 1912

Larrimore ......*Pasadena*, 1930

Larsen ....*Yellowstone*, 1928; *Chehalis*, 1930

Larson ....*Hartwood*, 1919; *F. S. Loop*, 1927–1930

Lass ....*Willamette*, 1919

Lauer ....*Fairhaven*, 1915

Lawless ....*Coos Bay*, 1884–1885

Lawson ....*Fair Oaks*, 1915

LeBouanic ......*Frank D. Stout*, 1926; *Necanicum*, 1927–1929

Lee ....*Noyo*, 1906–1907; *Sea Foam*, 1908; *Washington*, 1912

Levinson ....*Newsboy*, 1888; *Despatch*, 1904; *Johann Poulson*, 1906

Lewis ....*Brunswick*, 1936

Liebig ....*Sunol*, 1899

Lielsen ....*Mayfair*, 1928

Lilleland ....*Pomo*, 1908, 1912

Lind ....*Sea Foam*, 1924; *Brooklyn*, 1926–1927; *Florence Olson*, 1936–1937

Lindberg ....*Fifield*, 1915; *Northland*, 1919

Lindner ....*Arctic*, 1912–1919

Lindstedt ......*Solano*, 1914

Lofstrom ....*Del Norte*, 1907; *Mandalay*, 1908–1912

Lund ....*Celilo*, 1927–1930

Lundborg ......*Whitesboro*, 1887

Lundquist ......*Scotia*, 1899; *Newsboy*, 1900; *Ruth*, 1900; *Newberg*, 1904; *Rainier*, 1908

McClellan ......*North Fork*, 1900–1901; *F. A. Kilburn*, 1912

McClements ....*Brooklyn*, 1912

Macgenn ....*Arcata*, 1904

McGovern .....*Pasadena*, 1912; *Santa Monica*, 1927–1930

McKenzie ......*Scotia*, 1936

Madsen ....*Greenwood*, 1888; *Jewel*, 1898; *Luella*, 1900; *Samoa*, 1900, 1904–1908; *Cleone*, 1900, 1931; *Davenport*, 1931; *Unimak*, 1932–1936; *Elizabeth*, 1936–1937

Malmgren ......*Carlos*, 1919; *Katherine Donovan*, 1924

Malmstrom .....*Nome City*, 1924–1926

Marsen ....*Hornet*, 1912

Marshall ....*Arcata*, 1884–1888; *Alliance*, 1887

Appendix

Surname of Captain	Vessels Commanded and Years
Martensen	*Gualala*, 1908–1909; *Grays Harbor*, 1919
Martin	*Chico*, 1901, 1904; *Chehalis*, 1904; *Norwood*, 1904–1912
Mattsen	*Phoenix*, 1908; *Bertie M. Hanlon*, 1919; *Frank D. Stout*, 1927–1929; *Tiverton*, 1930; *Davenport*, 1931; *Elizabeth*, 1933–1935
Mattsson	*F. S. Loop*, 1913
Medeson	*Tiverton*, 1929
Meyer	*Willamette*, 1884
Michelsen	*G. C. Lindauer*, 1919
Mikkelsen	*Santiam*, 1919; *Flavel*, 1919
Miller	*Weott*, 1898; *Luella*, 1899–1900; *Point Arena*, 1904; *Sea Foam*, 1906; *Acme*, 1917–1919; *Daisy Freeman*, 1926
Minor	*Tillamook*, 1888
Mountfort	*Arcata*, 1887
Nason	*Washington*, 1906
Nelson	*Empire*, 1898, 1899–1900; *Arcata*, 1900–1904; *North Fork*, 1904–1912; *Arctic*, 1904–1906; *Ravalli*, 1906, 1912, 1915; *Yosemite*, 1912
Nicholson	*Newport*, 1888
Nielsen	*Davenport*, 1927–1930; *Mayfair*, 1927–1929; *Daisy Mitchell*, 1928; *Saginaw*, 1929; *San Antonio*, 1926
Nilson	*Daisy Freeman*, 1919
Nilsson	*Johann Poulson*, 1908
Nopander	*Coos Bay*, 1900; *Aurelia*, 1919
Norberg	*Celia*, 1904; *Brooklyn*, 1906
Nygram	*South Bay*, 1912
Nyman	*Albion*, 1912
Nynem	*Cleone*, 1915
Odesen	*Charles Nelson*, 1912
Odlund	*Phoenix*, 1904; *Vanguard*, 1908–1919
Olsen[6]	*Whitesboro*, 1900, 1904; *Brunswick*, 1900; *South Coast*, 1900, 1904; *Santa Monica*, 1904–1906; *Coquille River*, 1906; *Acme*, 1908; *Mayfair*, 1908; *Elizabeth*, 1908–1924; *Samoa*, 1912; *Jim Butler*, 1912, 1919; *Santa Monica*, 1915, 1919; *Northland*, 1926, 1927; *Quinault*, 1927–1931; *Wellesley*, 1927; *Prentiss*, 1927; *J. C. Kirkpatrick*, 1929–1930
Orsland	*Wapama*, 1919; *Everett*, 1926; *Willamette*, 1927
Panser	*Gualala*, 1904; *Temple E. Dorr*, 1908
Paton	*Humboldt*, 1884–1885
Patterson	*Willapa*, 1932
Paulson	*South Coast*, 1906; *Homer*, 1914; *Martha Buehner*, 1919
Payne	*Del Norte*, 1904–1906; *Olson & Mahoney*, 1908; *Necanicum*, 1919
Peterson	*Laguna*, 1898; *Newberg*, 1900; *Westport*, 1900; *Navarro*, 1901; *Washcalore*, 1909; *Trinidad*, 1919; *Cleone*, 1926; *Willamette*, 1930; *Willapa*, 1933; *Bandon*, 1936, 1937

[6] Midnight Olson was no doubt a superb skipper, but it is doubtful that he commanded all of these vessels. Yes, there probably were other Olsens, Olsons, and Ohlsons.

Surname of Captain	Vessels Commanded and Years

Pettersen ....*Johann Poulson*, 1919; *Tiverton*, 1930; *Yellowstone*, 1930, 1931; *Bertie M. Hanlon*, 1935

Pierce ....*Charles Nelson*, 1904

Poppe ....*Saginaw*, 1930–1931

Preble ....*Charles Nelson*, 1906

Ramselius ......*Riverside*, 1909

Reed ....*Arcata*, 1898–1900, 1907; *Mandalay*, 1901

Rees ....*Despatch*, 1912

Reiner ....*Willamette*, 1912–1915; *Nome City*, 1929

Reinertson ......*Pomo*, 1906; *Hoquiam*, 1908; *Tahoe*, 1919; *Vanguard*, 1924

Richardson .....*Greenwood*, 1907

Roberg ....*Rainier*, 1914; *G. C. Lindauer*, 1916; *Svea*, 1924–1930; *Oregon*, 1926–1927

Roberts ....*Surprise*, 1884; *South Coast*, 1912

Rosenblad ......*Bandon*, 1912–1919

Rosengren ......*Crescent City*, 1927; *San Antonio*, 1929–1932; *Svea*, 1929

Rustad ....*Newport*, 1927

Salt ....*Iaqua*, 1912

Samuelson ......*F. S. Loop*, 1919; *Necanicum*, 1924, 1926; *Fort Bragg*, 1929–1930; *Helen P. Drew*, 1933, 1935

Sandvig ....*Caoba*, 1924

Sanford ....*Mandalay*, 1906; *Del Norte*, 1912

Schage ....*Lakme*, 1900–1901

Schulter ....*Nome City*, 1927

Schultz ....*Daisy*, 1919; *Daisy Gadsby*, 1919–1933

Schillinsky .....*Prentiss*, 1907; *Bandon*, 1915

Sears ....*Rival*, 1906

Shea ....*Pomona*, 1900; *Coos Bay*, 1899

Shendahl ....*Cornelia*, 1936

Silvia ....*Yosemite*, 1919, 1924; *Wapama*, 1927

Simmons ......*Walla Walla*, 1885

Simonsen ......*Sea Foam*, 1919–1930; *Cleone*, 1929; *Vanguard*, 1930–1937

Smith ....*Newport*, 1884–1885; *Whitesboro*, 1888; *Eureka*, 1888; *Coos Bay*, 1888; *Mandalay*, 1904; *Daisy*, 1908–1912; *Daisy Gadsby*, 1912; *Daisy Mitchell*, 1922; *Pasadena*, 1919

Sohst ....*Homer*, 1919

Sorenson ....*South Bay*, 1907; *Shasta*, 1924; *Centralia*, 1924; *South Coast*, 1930; *Helen P. Drew*, 1933

Sparr ....*George L. Olson*, 1935

Stahlbaum .....*Sea Foam*, 1929; *Cottoneva*, 1932–1935

Stangeland .....*Rainier*, 1919

Stockfieth ......*Crescent City*, 1884–1901

Storrs ....*Mackinaw*, 1904

Stousland ......*Chehalis*, 1915

Sundman ......*G. C. Lindauer*, 1908–1912; *Oregon*, 1926

Svensen ....*Brooklyn*, 1913, 1915; *Centralia*, 1915–1916; *Alliance*, 1919; *Stanwood*, 1924, 1927

Appendix

Surname of Captain	Vessels Commanded and Years
Swanson	*Greenwood*, 1904; *Pomona*, 1904; *James S. Higgins*, 1912; *Multnomah*, 1926–1927
Swenson	*Stanwood*, 1919; *Barbara C*, 1926–1933; *Chehalis*, 1930
Tho	*Lassen*, 1924; *Shasta*, 1929, 1930
Thompson	*Cleone*, 1887; *Coquille River*, 1900
Tietjen	*Celilo*, 1919
Toutt	*Johann Poulson*, 1909
Tufversson	*Cleone*, 1919; *Helen P. Drew*, 1924–1929
Vartnaw	*Tahoe*, 1941
Von Helms	*Eureka*, 1884
Waagen	*Celilo*, 1935–1937
Walgren	*Brunswick*, 1912, 1919
Walvig	*Cleone*, 1898; *Newsboy*, 1900; *Scotia*, 1900; *Point Arena*, 1906; *Quinault*, 1912
Wehman	*Wasp*, 1906–1907; *Bee*, 1919
Westerholm	*Carlos*, 1927
Wetterquest	*Westport*, 1908
Wight	*Daisy Matthews*, 1926
Wilson	*Mukilteo*, 1929
Winkel	*Albion*, 1900; *Alcazar*, 1904–1906
Winter	*Barbara C*, 1928
Wyndham	*Mukilteo*, 1927
Zaddert	*South Coast*, 1899; *Santa Barbara*, 1908–1919; *Anne Hanify*, 1929

BIBLIOGRAPHY

ALLEY, BOWEN & COMPANY. *History of Marin County, History of Mendocino County, History of Sonoma County,* San Francisco, 1880.

BETTS, H. S. *Redwood,* United States Forestry Service, Washington, D.C., 1939.

BLEDSOE, A. J. *History of Del Norte County,* Eureka, 1881; *Indian Wars of the Northwest,* Bacon & Co., San Francisco, 1885.

CALIFORNIA STATE PRINTING OFFICE. *Forestry Handbook for the State of California,* 1943.

CARPENTER & MILBERRY. *History of Mendocino and Lake Counties,* Historical Record Company, Los Angeles, 1914.

CLEVERDON, W. T. *Pacific Coast Lumber Fleet—Coastwise,* San Francisco, 1925.

DAVIS, WILLIAM HEATH. *Seventy-five Years in California,* J. Howell, San Francisco, 1929.

GRAHAM, LIEUTENANT L. D., U.S.C.& G.S. *United States Coast Pilot, Pacific Coast,* United States Department of Commerce, Washington, D.C., 1934.

HARDING, P. N. *Across the Gangplank* in *The Log* (monthly), The Log Publications, San Francisco, 1933–1940.

JOY, OWEN C. *Humboldt Bay Region, 1850 to 1875,* California Historical Association, Los Angeles, 1929.

LEWIS & DRYDEN. *Maritime History of the Northwest Pacific,* Lewis & Dryden Printing Company, Portland, Oregon, 1895.

LLOYD'S REGISTER OF SHIPPING, *Lloyd's Register,* London, 1936 through 1940.

LEVIN, NAT. *Pacific Coast Ships and Trades,* Ship Owners' Association of the Pacific, San Francisco (monthly pamphlets, 1938 through 1941).

McNAIRN, J. C. *Steam Schooner Sagas,* United States Naval Institute Proceedings (Vol. 68, No. 7), Washington, D.C., 1942.

SHIP OWNERS' ASSOCIATION OF THE PACIFIC COAST. *Statistics of Steam Schooners of the Pacific Coast,* San Francisco, 1911 and 1913.

UNITED STATES DEPARTMENT OF COMMERCE. *Merchant Vessels of the United States,* Washington, D.C., 1906 through 1940.

UNITED STATES HYDROGRAPHIC OFFICE. *Wreck Information List,* Washington, D.C., 1945.

San Francisco City Directory, 1863 through 1920.

San Francisco Chronicle, Shipping pages, 1915 through 1930.

San Francisco Examiner, Shipping pages, 1878 through 1930.

INDEX

Index

153

Index

155